Peru

John Crabtree

Oxfam

First published by Oxfam GB in 2002

Available from:
Bournemouth English Book Centre, PO Box 1496, Parkstone,
Dorset, BH12 3YD, UK
tel: +44 (0)1202 712933; fax: +44 (0)1202 712930;
email: oxfam@bebc.co.uk

USA: Stylus Publishing LLC, PO Box 605, Herndon, VA
20172-0605, USA
tel: +1 (0)703 661 1581; fax: +1 (0)703 661 1547;
email: styluspub@aol.com

For details of local agents and representatives in other countries,
consult our website: http://www.oxfam.org.uk/publications
or contact Oxfam Publishing, 274 Banbury Road,
Oxford OX2 7DZ, UK
tel: +44 (0)1865 311 311; fax: +44 (0)1865 312 600;
email: publish@oxfam.org.uk

Our website contains a fully searchable database of all our titles,
and facilities for secure on-line ordering.

Oxfam GB is a registered charity, no. 202 918, and is a
member of Oxfam International.

© Oxfam GB 2002

ISBN 0 85598 482 1

A catalogue record for this publication is available from the
British Library.

Printed by
Information Press, Eynsham

Series designed by
Richard Morris, Stonesfield Design
Typeset in Scala and Gill Sans.

Contents

Peru and the Peruvians

The paradoxical co-existence of abundant natural wealth and pervasive human poverty is something that has struck generations of visitors to Peru. With its mineral reserves, oil, and gas, its fish resources, and its diverse agriculture, it is a country that should generate wealth for all to share. In reality, however, more than half of Peru's population earns less than the equivalent of two dollars a day. As the geographer Antonio Raimondi famously remarked, Peru is like a beggar seated on a bench of gold.

With their nose for gold and silver, the Spanish conquerors – or *conquistadores* – were swift to realise Peru's economic potential. From the mid-16th century onwards they turned Peru into the centre of an empire, the main function of which was to finance the Spanish crown's seemingly inexhaustible appetite for war. In the 19th century, following Peru's independence from Spain, the British and Americans – defying all geographical logic – built railways across the Andes in order to extract copper and silver from the mines of the Peruvian highlands, or *sierra*. More recently, foreign multinational companies have opened up new mining ventures, such as Yanacocha near Cajamarca, and Antamina in

◀ *Francisca Lama jokes with one of her many grandchildren. Like many other citizens, Francisca believes that the future of their town -- Tambo Grande in Piura -- is under threat from mining developments.*

▶ *Grass-roots organisations are increasingly demanding that their voices be heard throughout Peru. The women's groups taking part in this rally in Santo Domingo, Piura, were able to meet the mayor, and to present their proposals for change to him.*

Annie Bungeroth

Ancash, which mean that Peru will continue into the 21st century in its role as a supplier of minerals to the world market.

However, mining, and other extractive industries like fishing and hydrocarbons (oil and gas), have not produced a balanced pattern of development, either for Peru or for the majority of Peruvians. Although they generate export earnings, these economic activities produce little by way of employment or stimulus to other areas of the economy. This is the case today more than ever before. Mining, for instance, increasingly employs machinery rather than labour. Modern mining companies typically import technical know-how, and many of the other goods and services they require, as inputs. They do little to benefit the regions where they operate; rather, they frequently contaminate the rivers and divert precious water sources away from local agriculture and other uses.

Peru's governments have long wrestled with this paradox of wealth and poverty, but without success. In the late 1960s and early 1970s, a left-leaning military government nationalised foreign mining and oil interests, introduced a radical agrarian reform, and took steps to promote local industrialisation. It hoped that this would lead to a more balanced kind of development that would permit redistribution of wealth and income. It failed to do this, and instead it built up unpayable debts. Since then, governments have reverted to the more traditional export model, claiming that private initiative and individual property – not the state – will provide the most reliable means to extricate people from poverty. As this book will show, this is a view that is not entirely borne out by the facts.

Politically, Peru lacks a strong democratic tradition. For much of the 20th century it was ruled by authoritarian regimes, many of them military. The majority of the population lacked a political voice. The main party to express popular interests, the *Alianza Popular Revolucionaria Americana*, better known as APRA, aroused such distrust in elite circles that it was kept firmly at arm's length by successive governments, winning office only in 1985, over 60 years after it was first founded. In the late 1960s and early 1970s, the Peruvian military took it upon itself to break the power of the land-owning elite, paving the way towards greater social participation. The establishment of full democratic rights was only achieved in 1979, when those who were deemed illiterate (mostly indigenous people) finally won the right to vote.

▼ This stained glass in Lima city centre portrays the Spanish conquistadores.

Susana Pastor

In spite of this legacy of exclusion, the voice of ordinary people has gained strength over the years, often at the margins of the political system. An array of grass-roots organisations, rural as well as urban, has come to demand that their views and interests be taken on board by political leaders. Organisation runs deep in Peruvian political culture. In part, this reflects the strength of the peasant community, whose origins are rooted way back in Peru's pre-Hispanic past. A sense of community identity has persisted despite the best efforts of the *conquistadores* and their successors to erase it. Today, such organisation can make awkward demands on the country's rulers. It often jars with the activities of political parties and their leaders. It is patchy, stronger in some places than others. Its demands may be highly localised or very specific. Yet such popular organisation provides the bedrock on which a more genuine and participatory democracy can be built.

Who were the first Peruvians?

When the Spanish first arrived in Peru in 1532, they stumbled on one of the most sophisticated of all non-European civilisations. At its height, the Inca empire stretched some 4000 kilometres along the Andes, from what is now southern Colombia to northern Chile. Its population is reckoned to have exceeded 14 million. Through military conquest and administrative subordination, the Incas exercised control over a wide variety of ethnic groups, imposing a common religion and language (Quechua). Roads radiated from the capital, Cuzco, to the four corners of the empire, facilitating transport and communication. Cuzco was a magnificent city, with palaces reputedly decked in gold and silver. The foundations of these are still visible, as is the massive citadel of Sacsahuamán that overlooks the present-day city. Yet despite its size and sophistication, this was a civilisation that did not know the written word, the wheel, or the arch.

► *The ruins of Machu Picchu nestle in the foothills of the Andes. Hidden for many years, they were rediscovered in 1911, and have since become a major tourist attraction.*

Pat Wise

The Incas followed a long line of earlier Peruvian civilisations. The first conquest of the Andes is thought to have taken place some 20,000 years ago, and the remains of the earliest civilisations date from as far back as 11,000 BC. Various different cultures developed on the coast and in the Andes. Compared with some of its predecessors, the Inca civilisation was relatively short-lived. It first emerged in the valley of Cuzco in the 13th and 14th centuries, and entered its most expansive phase only under the Inca Pachacutí, less than a century before the Spanish arrived.

Apart from numerous spectacular ruins, important traces of the Incas still persist five centuries after its demise. The *ayllu*, the basic unit of Inca landholding, is still the foundation of agrarian society in the Andes. In the Inca *ayllu*, grazing land was held by the community while crop land was allotted to individual families according to their size, much as is the case today. Labour tasks, like ploughing or repairing irrigation ditches, were also carried out communally, distributed according to age and gender. This is still the norm in Peruvian peasant communities. With its complex systems of irrigation and terracing, Inca agriculture was able to sustain a population considerably larger than that which lives in the Peruvian Andes today.

The formation of modern Peru

The extent of modern Peru is defined by the way in which the Spanish empire broke up into separate jurisdictions prior to and during the wars of independence at the beginning of the 19th century. As the centre of colonial rule, Lima – known as the 'city of kings' – saw its influence dwindle during the 18th century. Peru was the last republic to be 'liberated', in 1821. A lack of definitive frontiers led to conflicts with its neighbours that have soured relations ever since. As a result of the War of the Pacific (1879-83), Chile annexed the provinces of Arica and Tarapacá. In 1932, Peru came to blows with Colombia over the border town of Leticia. In 1941, and again in 1995, there were wars with Ecuador over their disputed frontier. Recent governments have sought to resolve these issues, and since 1969 Peru has been a member of the Andean Pact alongside Chile (which withdrew in 1975), Bolivia, Ecuador, Colombia, and Venezuela. Still, border problems have yet to be buried entirely. As the 1995 war with Ecuador showed, they can sometimes resurface with surprising force and in unexpected ways.

A fractured landscape

Range after range of bare, jagged ridges rise up out of the coastal mist. The landscape is the texture and colour of crumpled parchment, devoid of human inprint but for a thin black line, way below. This is the road up to Ayacucho from Pisco on the coast. It loops this way and that as it pushes upwards towards the high mountain plains, or *puna*. The line of the

Annie Bungeroth

cordillera, the watershed between the Amazon and the Pacific, is etched with light, dusty snow. To the east, the sun's rays throw darts of light across this vast, barren terrain, as the land begins to slope downwards, brown turning to ochre and grey, and eventually with hints of green. Whether seen from the air on the morning flight from Lima to Ayacucho, or traversed by road or even railway, the Andes are the defining feature of Peru's uncompromising geography, a wall that separates cultures and peoples, an obstacle both to economic integration and to the development of a single sense of nation.

Most Peruvians now live on the coast, or *costa*, a narrow strip of inhospitable brown desert bisected by fertile valleys, irrigated by the rivers that descend from the *cordillera*. The city of Lima, along with the port of Callao, has a population of over 8 million. It is home to nearly one third of all Peruvians. Several of Peru's other major cities are built on or near the coast. On the face of it, it is odd that Peru's main centres of population have grown up in areas where there is so little water or natural vegetation. Nothing grows in the coastal deserts unless water is brought from elsewhere, and even in the coastal river valleys, water supply is seasonal and dependent on rainfall in the sierra. Despite this, the coastal deserts are full of the remains of pre-Columbian civilisations that managed to flourish in spite of the lack of water. According to one of the more plausible theories, the mysterious Nazca lines were a sophisticated method of identifying potential water sources. Situated to the south of Lima, they consist of vast geometric patterns and outlines of animal forms, etched into the desert sands.

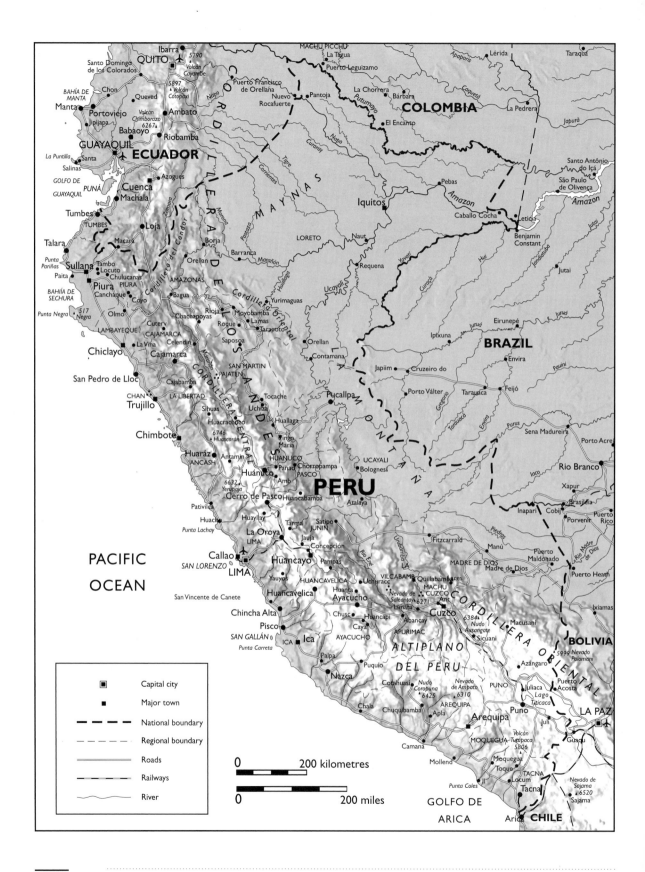

PACIFIC
OCEAN

COLOMBIA

BRAZIL

PERU

BOLIVIA

ECUADOR

CHILE

GOLFO DE
ARICA

Legend

◻	Capital city
■	Major town
▬ ▬ ▬	National boundary
– – –	Regional boundary
═══	Roads
▬▬▬	Railways
∼∼∼	River

0   200 kilometres

0   200 miles

▶ *Gathering salt from the Sechura desert, on the north-west coast of Peru. The salt mine is owned by the peasant community of Sechura, and profits are shared with all community members.*

The river valleys are oases of vegetation. A thin irrigation ditch is often all that separates brown from green, a frontier between ecosystems. The valleys have long provided food for the citizens of Lima, as well as export cash-crops such as cotton, sugar, and latterly 'niche' products like asparagus. Rich coastal estates were among the areas affected by the 1970s agrarian reform, when they were converted into co-operatives. The agricultural possibilities of the coast have since been enhanced by massive and costly public investment projects that use lengthy aquaducts to bring water to the coast from the high Andes. In the case of the Majes project, near Arequipa, the headwaters of the Amazon were diverted and channelled westward through the *cordillera* to irrigate the coastal desert plains. As a result of this hugely expensive project, Majes has the distinction of producing some of the most costly alfalfa the world has ever known.

The arid climate of coastal Peru and Chile is a result of the Andes blocking the moist trade winds that blow westwards across South America from the Atlantic. The prevailing winds blow in from the Pacific instead, whilst temperatures are moderated by the cold Humboldt ocean current that flows northwards from Antarctica to the tropical latitudes off Ecuador. A low-lying coastal mist is normally the only source of humidity. The Humboldt is a branch of a cold current that flows eastwards at latitudes close to Antarctica, and then turns north up the coast of Chile and Peru. The cold water brings with it nitrates and phosphates from the seabed, generating abundant plankton and thus a wealth of fish. Every few years, however, the Humboldt is displaced by a warm current that flows southward from the tropics. This is the *El Niño* ('boy child') phenomenon, named by the fishermen after the baby Jesus because the increase in sea temperatures is first noted around Christmas time. Rather than seasonal blessings, *El Niño* disrupts the climate. It raises the sea temperature, killing the plankton that bring the fish. It brings rainfall where normally

► The El Niño of 1997-98 caused widespread flooding in many parts of Peru. These boys, from Chulucanas in Piura, are showing how far up the walls of their home the flood waters rose.

Annie Bungeroth

there is none, causing floods and landslides. And it wreaks havoc in the highlands, or *sierra*, causing drought in places where agriculture is critically dependent on regular annual rainfall.

The precipitous steeps of the sierra, with its splintered sides of porphyry and granite, and its higher regions wrapped in snows that never melt under the fierce sun of the equator, unless it be from the desolating action of its own volcanic fires, might seem equally unpropitious to the labours of the husbandman. And all communication between the parts of the long-extended territory might be thought to be precluded by the savage character of the region, broken up by precipices, furious torrents, and impassable quebradas – *those hideous rents in the mountain chain, whose depths the eye of the terrified traveller, as he winds along his aerial pathway, vainly endeavours to fathom.*

(Prescott: History of the Conquest of Peru)

Across the Andes and into the Amazon

Lying between the western and eastern ranges of the Andes, the inter-Andean valleys were once the cradle of the Inca civilisation and its precursors. These valleys have traditionally been Peru's main bread basket, as well as the source of most of its mineral wealth. During the colonial period many cities grew up in the sierra, notably Cuzco, but also Cajamarca, Huaraz, Huancayo, and Ayacucho. Mainly peopled by Spanish immigrants, such cities grew rich on the commerce spawned by mining. By far the most important mine was Potosí, situated in what is now Bolivia, whose silver was carried overland to Lima and thence by galleon to Spain. Labour for the mines came from the indigenous population, who were forced to work in inhuman conditions by their Spanish masters. Since the 19th century, the economy of the *sierra* has stagnated. It has been bypassed by the development that has occurred in Lima and on the coast. With its ornate colonial churches and once aristocratic mansions, Ayacucho is a striking reminder of a vanished Peru.

From pre-Inca times, peoples have farmed in the Andes. Traditionally, communities would offset the risks inherent in peasant agriculture by farming at many different altitudes. Today, some communities farm at over 4000 metres above sea level. Notwithstanding this diverse approach to farming, good land with access to water is in short supply. Until the 1969 agrarian reform, such land was concentrated in the hands of exploitative landlords, known as *gamonales*. Though the reform fragmented the landed estates, it failed to resolve the problems of peasant farming. As we shall see further on, subsistence peasant farmers in the *sierra* remain the poorest of the poor in Peru.

Where the Andes fall away to the east, land and rainfall become plentiful, and entirely different ecosystems emerge. Steep-sided valleys lead downwards to the sub-tropical lowlands, known as the 'high jungle' (or *selva alta*) where, in recent years, coca – the raw material for cocaine – has been king. Most of these areas were opened up to inward migration only in the second half of the 20th century. They were colonised by farmers from the *sierra*, many released from feudal-style bonds by the agrarian reform, and attracted to the *selva* by its agricultural potential. But this inward migration was at the expense of lowland indigenous peoples, whose lands were progressively encroached upon. Conflicts over land led to clashes, often violent, between settlers and indigenous people.

The foothills of the Andes eventually give way to the flat Amazon jungle (*selva baja*). From the air, it looks like a carpet of green, broken only by the wide, red-brown, meandering rivers that form the Amazon river system. Although it constitutes half of the country's surface area, the Amazon jungle is home to less than five per cent of Peru's population. Its main city, Iquitos, situated just below the point where the waters of the Ucayali and Marañon rivers merge to form the Amazon proper, is still only accessible from the rest of Peru by air or river boat. This jungle is one of the most biologically diverse regions on the planet.

So far, the Peruvian Amazon has been less affected by deforestation than neighbouring Brazil. Nevertheless, its rich natural resources mean it is just as vulnerable to uncontrolled exploitation. The lowland Indians, whose lifestyle is perilously dependent on the environment, are threatened by the inroads of outsiders, whether highland migrants, logging firms, oil and gas companies, or those who come to pan gold.

From coastal deserts, to high mountains, to equatorial rainforest, Peru incorporates a vast range of different ecosystems and micro-climates. It is a hotspot for biodiversity. Peru ranks eighth in the world for the diversity of its flowering plants. Yet, as we shall see, many of Peru's fragile ecologies are increasingly under threat as a result of the development of unsustainable extractive industries.

▼ *This statue stands in the centre of Lamas, a town on the edge of the Amazon jungle. It portrays a* conquistador *and a native Indian shaking hands, purporting to represent the 'meeting and friendship' between the two cultures.*

Susana Pastor

Winners and losers in a fractured society

On one side lies Monterico, one of Lima's most affluent suburbs; on the other, Pamplona, a city of the poor. A high wall separates the two, arrayed with spikes and broken glass. The wall is a frontier between two worlds, a symbol of social separation and division. Constructed as a line of defence against land invasions, for the citizens of Monterico it acts like a dike stemming the rising tide of poverty; for those in Pamplona it is a physical reminder of the seemingly insurmountable barriers to social advancement.

Despite having adopted republican values nearly two centuries ago, Peru remains a very unequal society. The cutting of its links with imperial Spain did not bring major changes in social structure; rather, it reinforced the dominance of a local elite. Unlike some countries in Latin America – such as Mexico, Bolivia, or Cuba – Peru has never experienced a social revolution from below. Alexander von Humboldt, the German geographer who gave his name to the ocean current, is said to have marvelled at the differences he observed between rich and poor when he studied the country at the beginning of the 19th century. Peru today is almost as unequal as it was in Humboldt's day, causing some to ask how such deep inequality can be perpetuated over such long periods of time.

Inequality also exists between men and women, particularly in terms of access to privilege and power. The numbers of women visible in public life, whether in politics or business, are still very few. Although women have increasingly challenged this in recent years, *machismo* (the traditional pattern of male dominance) remains deeply ingrained in Peruvian culture. Peruvian women earn, on average, 46 per cent less than men. They usually work in less secure occupations. They are more likely to be

▲ *Collecting brazil nuts amid the lush vegetation of the Peruvian Amazon. It takes 25 years before a brazil nut tree begins to bear fruit. The trees have an average life-span of 100 years.*

AC Gonzales Vigil

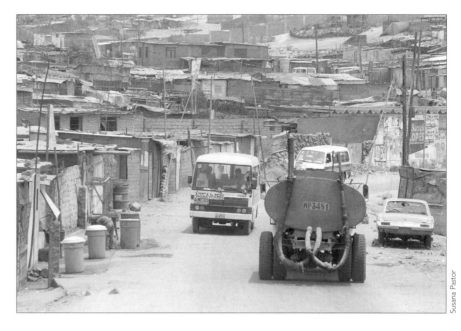

▶ Each phase of new building in Pamplona Alta, one of Lima's poorest suburbs, takes the makeshift houses further away from essential basic services like electricity, water, and sanitation. The water truck passing through the street sells water at some of the highest prices in Lima.

Susana Pastor

▼ Traditionally, men and women perform different kinds of work in Peru. Women are more likely than men to be responsible for household tasks like child-care. Marcos and his family are unusual. His wife earns money washing clothes, while he stays at home and looks after their children.

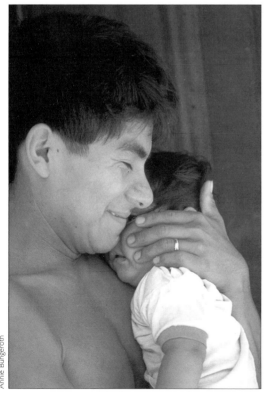

Annie Bungeroth

illiterate than men (especially in rural areas), and to have received less formal education. Although women head around a quarter of all Peruvian households, notions of male dominance persist within the family. Yet life in Peru has not always been like this. In Inca times, although there was a division of labour between men and women, there was much more equality between the sexes than there is today. Women and men shared the resources of the *ayllu*, and women could inherit property from their mothers. Patriarchy really arrived with the Spanish *conquistadores*, whose traditions of male inheritance and dominance transformed Peruvian society.

Regional and ethnic identities are another source of division in Peruvian society. Such divisions reinforce social barriers, making it even harder to clear the 'wall' of social advancement. The pattern of regional development in recent decades has been to favour the coast over the *sierra* and *selva*, to favour cities at the expense of rural areas, and, above all, to favour Lima. Successive governments have paid lip-service to the notion of decentralisation, but have not succeeded in redressing these imbalances. This has led to high levels of internal migration, especially towards Lima, which has exacerbated the situation still further. Regions outside Lima are now coming to demand a larger share of public spending, and a bigger say in how it is distributed.

Escaping from poverty – 'one step forward, two steps back'?

Peru has some of the highest levels of poverty of any Latin American country. More than half of the population lives in poverty. These citizens receive incomes lower than the officially-defined poverty line, as measured by the cost of a basket of food and other vital consumer items. Of these, nearly half again live in 'extreme poverty', with income insufficient to buy even the most essential food items. There are seven million people whose incomes are thus insufficient to meet the most basic needs. This acute poverty goes hand-in-hand with other key symptoms of deprivation, such as high infant mortality, high illiteracy rates, and low life expectancy.

Nearly three quarters of Peruvians living in rural areas are classified as 'poor', and just over half as 'extremely poor'. Subsistence farmers in the *sierra* are particularly affected. These households depend on the food that they themselves can grow, and they generate little cash income. However, while poverty is more acute in rural areas, it is also widespread in urban centres. In Lima, for example, 40 per cent of the population lives in poverty, mainly in the slum areas that spread out from the centre towards the city's hinterland. The main problem here is unemployment, and what is sometimes called 'under-employment'. In Lima, the unemployed and under-employed account for 60 per cent of the potential workforce. The under-employed consist of the self-employed, and those who work in 'informal' firms who enjoy none of the legal protection and other benefits of proper employment. Under-employment is indeed a misnomer: in order to survive, most people in this category work long hours in a variety of low-paid occupations. With no unemployment benefits, few can afford to be unemployed for long.

► Tania Mamani concentrates on her homework amid the building rubble. She lives in San Juan de Lurigancho, Lima's most densely populated neighbourhood. In this district, 44 per cent of the population has no water, 49 per cent has no sanitation, and 27 per cent of the children under six are malnourished. It is difficult for people here to find paid employment, and make a living.

Annie Bungeroth

The quest for social improvement is a strong driving force among the poor. Every night, many thousands of people attend night-school to acquire basic skills and qualifications. Education is one of the few avenues for social advancement in Peru. However, job opportunities for skilled and qualified people are limited, and only the lucky few find a route out of poverty this way. Even university graduates struggle to find formal sector employment: the number of university-trained taxi drivers in Lima attests to this.

The only time in recent memory when social advancement for the poor became a reality was in the 1960s and early 1970s, when the expansion of the public sector brought with it large numbers of reasonably well-paid jobs, nurturing Peru's small middle class. With the reversal of such policies in the 1980s and 1990s, this avenue was blocked.

Ethnic diversity: source of conflict and creativity

Peru is a rich mixture of different cultures and languages. In the *sierra*, the main indigenous tongue is Quechua, the language of the Incas. In the vicinity of Lake Titicaca, on the frontier with Bolivia, people speak Aymara, an unrelated language. In the jungle, there are more than 60 different indigenous peoples, grouped into 14 linguistic families.

Although the precise boundaries between ethnic groups have been blurred by migration and inter-marriage, especially in urban areas, there remains a fairly close association between social position and skin colour in Peru: the darker your skin, the lower your status. Racism is omnipresent, reinforcing social divides. Ethnic exclusion has, however, generated less political tension in Peru than in neighbouring Ecuador or Bolivia. In part, this is because the agrarian reform broke with predominant ideas about ethnic identity, known as *indigenismo*, that sought to glorify the Inca past. It officially abolished the remnants of serfdom in rural areas and raised the status of the peasant farmer or *campesino*. It thus opened up alternative paths towards 'modernity' and 'citizenship'. At the same time, José Carlos Mariátegui, the founding father of Peruvian Marxism, reinterpreted *indigenismo* as expressing class struggle, not ethnic division. All this is not to say that ethnicity does not form an important part in defining modern Peruvian identities; it helps to explain the persistence of indigenous languages, beliefs, and customs. Ethnic pride reinforces identities in regional centres like Cuzco, Huancavelica, and Ayacucho. But such identities are not usually defined by ethnicity alone.

Where ethnic consciousness is perhaps most evident and forthright is among the lowland Amazon Indians, for whom defence of their territory and of their way of life are one and the same. The lowland Indians are notoriously circumspect in their dealings with the Peruvian state, keeping their distance from political parties of all sorts – as a result of which they have scant representation in national politics. They are distrustful of mainstream politicians, and feel encroached-upon by outsiders, both

OUT OF THE MELTING POT – EMERGING IDENTITIES

Peru's ethnic boundaries are increasingly being blurred by migration and inter-marriage, or *mestizaje* (mixing). This is creating a new class of 'mixed' people, or *cholos*, building new identities. There is no fixed definition of '*cholo*', and the term is the subject of controversy among anthropologists. Essentially, *cholos* are people who by moving from their place of origin no longer belong anywhere. They are neither fully accepted in their new habitat, nor in the place they have left behind. *Cholo* has traditionally been a pejorative term. However, the numbers of *cholos* in Peru today mean that such notions of rejection and stigma have had to be revised. In Lima, and other large cities, *cholos* are now the majority. For many, to be *cholo* has become a source of pride and even cultural affirmation. *Choloficación* has became the principal way in which indigenous identities are being 'modernised', and creatively re-interpreted.

migrants from the highlands, and others who seek to exploit the natural resources of the jungle. The relationship between lowland Indians and these incomers is often one of suspicion, and even violence.

A culture 'of all bloods'

Although it can be the source of conflicts, Peru's geographic, regional, and ethnic diversity is the key to the country's vibrant popular culture, a culture that also reflects a strong sense of community and history. It is a culture, to borrow Arguedas's famous phrase, 'of all bloods' (*de todas las sangres*), a culture that has produced a rich mixture of dance, music, stories, painting, and craftsmanship. This living, dynamic culture constantly adopts, and adapts to, new influences. Traditions are thus transferred to Lima and the coast, where they are changed and developed, but not lost. Culture thus continuously provides a way of linking past, present, and future in endlessly creative ways. It also provides a way of reasserting community or even ethnic pride in ways that reinforce the bonds that join people together. *Chicha*, a music of the urban slums, is but one of the more recent variants of this cultural mixing. *Chicha* music is a hybrid of the modern, tropical *cumbia* from Colombia, and traditional Peruvian *huayno* rhythms.

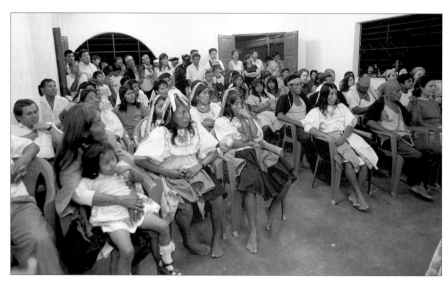

► The people of Lamas attend the launch of two books about biodiversity and reforestation in the Amazon. The native Aguaruna community at Lamas still retains many traditional customs, as well as the local dialect.

Susana Pastor

► Around 200 family members will attend the Pérez family fiesta, in homage to the Virgin, 'Mama Limpia'. The women are preparing the food for the three-day fiesta. Networks of family members, friends, and neighbours come together in order to guarantee the costs of the fiesta. Without these networks, fiestas would be impossible.

Susana Pastor

Fiesta! Building community through celebration

The fiesta, the annual celebration of the local patron saint, is the key date in the calendar for all Peruvian communities. Fiestas can last for days – even as long as a week. Despite their sacred and religious importance, fiestas are not solemn occasions. Typically, they include days and nights of parades, music, dancing, and plentiful drinking. They place high demands on all citizens – fiestas are expensive, and every community member must help in the organisation of the event, as well as participating to the full in the fun. But the costs and benefits of the fiesta cannot be calculated in narrow economic terms. The fiesta is an investment in the intangible, in the future of the community.

► Saint's day at Catacaos – townspeople are making ready for the religious procession.

Susana Pastor

Religious devotions underscore everyday activities, and are fused into a cultural tradition that is by no means wholeheartedly Christian. Festivals of various kinds at different times of the year provide constant reminders of the depth of popular religiosity. Yet although the Catholic Church remains a powerful institution, closely linked to the state, it no longer enjoys the undisputed power it once wielded. As in other countries, modern life in Peru is increasingly secular, and though the majority of Peruvians have been baptised as Catholics, the numbers who attend mass regularly are dwindling. The Catholic Church is experiencing great problems in recruiting enough priests to fill its parishes. It is also confronting a major challenge from a variety of evangelical Protestant churches. These have grown rapidly in recent years, their message and approach often more appealing to the poor than those of traditional Catholicism. Moreover, within the Catholic Church deep chasms have emerged between priests committed to social transformation, and a hierarchy that is ever more conservative. The present Archbishop of Lima, Juan Luis Cipriani, was the first-ever cardinal anywhere to belong to Opus Dei, a right-wing ecclesiastical movement which has origins in fascist Spain.

▼ *Baptism in Ayacucho*

Susana Pastor

► Baldomero Alejos (1924-76) was one of Peru's most famous photographers. Viewing his pictures at this exhibition was a way for Peruvians to explore their memories of the past. Graciela Romero Sulca points to the picture of herself, her brother, her mother, and grandmother: 'I was only 12 years old…. The others are dead now, and I am the only one still alive. I've lived to be 74 – it's amazing! What a wonderful photograph!'

Susana Pastor

MADE IN PERU

The many faces of Peru and Peruvian culture are the subject of 'Hecho en el Perú' ('Made in Peru'), a piece of drama written to celebrate the 30th anniversary of the experimental theatre group, Yuyachkani. Yuyachkani wants to create theatrical experiences that ordinary people can relate to and enjoy. 'Hecho en el Perú' was free to all, and staged in the heart of old Lima, so that the event would reach as many people as possible.

'Hecho en el Perú' stretches theatrical conventions to the limit to create new forms of audience involvement. It takes the public on a stroll through six interactive scenes, each acted out behind a glass screen. The audience can spend as long or as little as it wishes in front of each one. Each contains a single actor who explores an important theme in contemporary Peruvian culture. The scenes place the lives of ordinary people at the heart of the theatrical experience. 'La Madre Patria' ('The Mother Country') is an ironic exploration of the creation of myths about 'nationhood', and the way in which these are used to prop up a status quo that keeps the majority of Peruvians in poverty. It ridicules the formal symbols of republicanism, and looks askance at other cultural forces, such as the Catholic Church, and the influence of Spain and Japan. Another scene, 'Pieles de Mujer' (literally, 'Woman's Skins') explores the many different roles of women in Peruvian society: the campesina with her coca, the young militant guerrilla fired up by Maoist doctrine, the woman press-ganged into paramilitary activities by the army, the mother, the maid, the protesting mineworker's wife, and the nun. 'Desembarque' ('Disembarking') examines the life of Peruvian emigrés, the humiliations they have to suffer in seeking acceptance in a new country, and their nostalgia for the home they have left behind. Other themes are explored in equally creative ways.

Yuyachkani means 'I am remembering' in Quechua. According to Miguel Rubio, one of Yuyachkani's original founders, and the director of 'Hecho en el Perú', 'Memory of the past, and how it informs the present, has to provide the key to a better future.'

Displaced people

Beyond the limits of upper- and middle-class Lima neighbourhoods like Miraflores, San Isidro, and Monterico, most of the city's straggling suburbs began as rows of flimsy shacks erected in the desert sands, or on the barren and rocky mountainsides that protrude like fingers from the Andean foothills towards the ocean. Today, many of these once precarious shanties are densely populated townships with buildings four and five storeys high. This is a tribute to the tenacity of the original settlers of 30 or 40 years ago: they have created a new society out of nothing. It is a world that is far from static: the roofs of most buildings sprout the iron rods of unfinished reinforced concrete pillars, signs of new floors to come. In the outer reaches of the metropolis, ever further from the historic centre, new makeshift shacks of reed panels (*esteras*) appear every week as the city's latest wave of residents dig in.

Above all, Lima is a migrant city. For at least 50 years it has attracted people from the *sierra* with a promise of modernity, wealth, and social advancement. Back in the 1950s, Peru's population was one-third urban and two-thirds rural; by the 1990s, it was the other way round. Many neighbourhoods have developed by attracting people from the same place of origin, helping to reproduce in the city the diverse cultures of rural Peru. Those who are already established can provide a helping hand to newcomers, whether friends, relatives, or *paisanos* – people from the areas they originally hailed from. Regional and local clubs keep the spirit of the Andes alive within the dust, bricks, and concrete of this very different reality.

The city continues to attract migrants from all over the country, in large part because of the extremes of poverty that still prevail in much of rural Peru. For the young and enterprising in particular, Lima offers a more promising future than tilling the land for scant return. The explosive growth of Lima and other cities is a symptom of the failure of successive governments to improve the prospects for agriculture, especially among peasants and other small farmers. While the agrarian reform was designed to provide a new deal for the peasant by giving access to land, it also failed to provide the markets, credit, and other necessary inputs required to make peasant agriculture economically viable. Significantly, the fastest period of migration to Lima and other coastal cities took place during the decade following the enactment of the agrarian reform.

Susana Pastor

▲ *Modesto helps his neighbour Oscar to rebuild the walls of his house in Catacaos. They will cover the tall reed panels with wet mud, which will dry solid in the sun.*

Annie Bungeroth

▲ *Tawaq is a ceramics workshop in Lima. Its members fled from Ayacucho in the Andes, to escape the fighting. They started out with nothing, living in temporary shelters on the edge of Lima. Today, members of the workshop, like Virginia and her son Irwin, earn a good living and have invested in their homes and the business.*

▼ *Influences from abroad – Harry Potter arrives in Lima.*

Susana Pastor

Migration in Peru is also a product of political violence and forced displacement. In the savage guerrilla war that raged in the Andes during the 1980s and early 1990s, peasants found themselves caught in the crossfire between *Sendero Luminoso* (the guerrilla fighters) and the military. The conflict led to the depopulation of large areas of the *sierra*, especially in the southern-central departments of Ayacucho, Huancavelica, and Apurímac. With Sendero effectively controlling large swathes of the Andes, it became impossible for peasant farmers and their families to continue tending the land. At the same time, they also suffered brutal reprisals from the military. Large numbers fled to the relative safety of towns and cities, many eventually finding their way to the most recent shanties on the periphery of Lima. In the highlands around Ayacucho, the ruined remnants of deserted villages stand as stark reminders to the devastating effects of this violence on rural life. Despite the organisation of programmes to assist people to return to their communities once the violence had abated, only a small proportion have chosen to embark on the arduous task of rebuilding from scratch their destroyed peasant livelihoods and communities.

Over the last 20 years, Peruvians have moved ever further afield in the search for a better future. No-one knows for sure how many are living in other countries, but estimates range as high as 2.5 million, or 9 per cent of the total population of Peru. Peruvian emigrants are scattered through a wide range of countries in Latin America, North America, Europe, and even as far away as Japan, Korea, and Australia. The two countries with the largest Peruvian colonies are the USA and Spain. Wherever they have settled, most migrants have entered illegally, trapped in a world of semi-informality and legal insecurity.

Up until the 1970s, the only Peruvians to settle abroad were the well-to-do who went away to study, or those exiled for political reasons. Since then, most have belonged to lower income groups, although they are not usually the poorest of the poor. The majority are young, and many have received secondary education of some sort. Their motives for migrating vary, but economic necessity is by far the most important. Although they may cling to their Peruvian identity and customs, few, having made the break, think of returning, except possibly for holidays or to visit relatives. However, the money that migrants send back to their families each year, estimated at $1.2 billion, is probably more than the revenue that Peru earns from copper, its most important export commodity. Peru's main export is therefore its people. This exodus of young people, many with education and skills, represents a haemorrhage of potential talent, a human brain drain.

THE *HUAYNO* – MELANCHOLY MUSIC OF THE *SIERRA*

Few dance rhythms are more typical of the Peruvian *sierra* than the *huayno*. *Huaynos* from Ayacucho have a reputation for being particularly melancholy. Usually played on the harp, violin, and guitar, the songs often speak about the relation between man and nature, and reflect the poverty and hardship typical in Ayacucho. They involve a sharing of grief and personal suffering, as well as a sense of community and brotherhood. In recent years, the *huayno* has achieved fame, regionally, nationally, and even internationally. Such fame is a source of pride for Andean communities, whose bands compete for recognition. In part, their success is a consequence of the struggle for human rights in Ayacucho. Many contemporary *huaynos* relate to violence and forced migration, problems that have impressed themselves on the country as a whole. There are thousands of *huayno* groups, hundreds in Ayacucho alone, interpreting and reinterpreting their individual and social predicament through music.

Susana Pastor

▲ 'El Trio los Cuatro' (the 'Trio of Four') has been playing together in Ayacucho for over 15 years. They will play for the three days of the Pérez family fiesta, resting for only two or three hours each day.

Huérfano Pajarillo
(Popular *huayno* from Ayacucho)

Ayacuchano huérfano pajarillo
A qué has venido a tierras extrañas
Alza tu vuelo, vamos a Ayacucho
Donde tus padres lloran tu ausencia

En tu pobre casa no te ha faltado
Caricias, delicias, demás has tenido
Sólo la pobreza con su tiranía
Entre sus garras quiso oprimirte

Little orphan bird
Ayacuchano, little orphan bird
Why have you flown to distant parts?
Spread your wings, let's go to Ayacucho
Where your family weeps for your absence.

In your humble home you've never lacked
Affection, delights you've had aplenty
Only poverty with its tyranny
Has tried to oppress you in its claws.

The fight for democracy

Susana Pastor

▲ *América Television was directly implicated in the corrupt activities of Fujimori's government. Today, the company is fighting to retain its transmission signal.*

Fujimori and the 'Vladivideos'

Never before has a video brought down a regime. On 14 September 2000, just six weeks after being sworn in for a third consecutive period of office, President Alberto Fujimori's closest adviser, Vladimiro Montesinos, was shown on prime-time television – watched by millions of Peruvians – handing wads of money to a newly-elected opposition congressman, Alex Kouri, to lure him into supporting the government. In the weeks that followed, several more such videos were screened on national television, showing Montesinos handing out cash to bribe prominent judges, journalists, media-owners, and businessmen. It became clear to all just how Peru had been governed in the ten years since Fujimori first became president in 1990, and the lengths to which Montesinos had gone to mount the fraud that secured Fujimori's second re-election in 2000. The 'Vladivideos', as they became known, opened people's eyes. 'It was more brazen than any of us had ever imagined,' says Federico Arnillas, the head of the *Asociación Nacional de Centros* (ANC), an umbrella organisation for Peruvian NGOs, 'It was power in its most naked form.'

Within just over two months of the Kouri video being shown, Fujimori had left the country, and Montesinos was in hiding in Venezuela, soon to be arrested and returned to Peru. Fujimori sought refuge in Japan, his ancestral home; ironically, Montesinos ended up in the Callao naval base, in a jail complex he had himself designed to accommodate Abimael Guzmán, the founder and leader of Sendero Luminoso. An interim administration – hastily assembled and presided over by an otherwise unassuming congressman, Valentín Paniagua – launched a return to democracy, and announced fresh presidential and congressional elections. The dismantling of the Fujimori system of government had begun, bringing with it the arrest of key figures associated with the regime, including senior members of the armed forces.

Susana Pastor

▲ *Students from the military college in Piura. Traditionally, the military provided a ladder for social advancement. Today, however, its role in society is severely questioned.*

From coups to loos: the rise and fall of Fujimori

Fujimori was a political unknown when he clinched the presidency in 1990. His only claim to fame at the time was that he had once been rector of the Agrarian University. His election represented a rejection of politicians and the political class, and in particular of Mario Vargas Llosa – the world-famous writer – who had headed up a right-wing coalition, and who most pundits thought would win.

Fujimori, the son of Japanese migrants, snatched victory without a political party to back him up, without funds to finance a presidential campaign, without powerful backers in the business community, and without campaign advisers to guide his every turn. He was elected on the disarmingly simple slogan of 'honesty, technology, and hard work', values that many Peruvians supposed to be typically Japanese.

Within two years of taking office, Fujimori had shown his mettle as a political operator. He seized the initiative in overcoming the hyperinflation he had inherited from his predecessor, Alan García. Taking advantage of the popularity this brought, he turned the tables on his political adversaries by closing down Congress, suspending the Supreme Court, and abolishing regional assemblies. He then held fresh congressional elections, this time winning the parliamentary majority he had lacked previously. In turn, this paved the way to a rewriting of the constitution, and the removal of the bar on his immediate presidential re-election. Fujimori's third political 'coup' in these years was the capture of Guzmán and the dismantling of Sendero Luminoso. Buoyed up by these successes, and constantly distancing himself from what he called the '*partidocracia*' (Peru's traditional party politicians), Fujimori set about maintaining power for the long haul.

In this he had a key ally in the armed forces. Alarmed by the escalation of political violence and what it saw as the economic irresponsibility of the García government, in 1988 the army High Command had produced a document, known as 'The Green Book'. This underlined the need for a lengthy period – 15 years or more – of firm, authoritative government, in order to end guerrilla subversion and to engineer the shift to a more liberal economy. Though few had ever heard of Fujimori at the time the document was written, it provided the blueprint that his government would follow. One of the key links between Fujimori and the military in the early days was Montesinos, a former army captain who had been dismissed during the left-wing military regime of the early 1970s for selling secrets to the CIA. Having won Fujimori's confidence, Montesinos set about building up a formidable intelligence machine, the National Intelligence Service, or SIN. The SIN was to become the regime's ears and eyes, the department responsible for covert activities.

The other two feet of the 'tripod' of power were the business community and popular opinion. With hyperinflation under control, and growth restored, businessmen began to support Fujimori. The government's radical programme of privatisation, which included mines, banks, telecommunications companies, and utilities, provided ample opportunity for lucrative business deals. Its 'no-nonsense' approach to organised labour also won plaudits among the economic elite. However, without public opinion on his side, Fujimori would have been unable to sustain himself in power for long. His landslide re-election victory in 1995, though marred by some irregularities, was a personal triumph. Fujimori's popularity ratings remained high. The lack of serious electoral opposition appears to have convinced him of his chances of winning again in 2000, despite the doubtful constitutionality of a second re-election. It was only in 1998 and 1999 that his popularity began to ebb.

To help build popular support, Fujimori had launched an anti-poverty programme, revamping the Ministry of the Presidency as the main conduit for funds. As its name suggests, the ministry became closely associated with Fujimori himself. It sought to bypass local government and the traditional spending ministries like transport, education, and health, and to channel funds directly to where they were most needed. The system was designed to leave people in no doubt as to who their benefactor was. Throughout the country, large orange hoardings (orange being Fujimori's electoral colours) were intended to convey the impression that the president was labouring day and night in the interests of the poor. Even today, orange-coloured latrines – we could call them 'Fujiloos' (in Spanish they are called *fujisilos*) – dot the landscape in rural areas, a curious reminder of a disgraced ex-president. But his popular campaign was not just a matter of latrines and public works. Food assistance programmes multiplied, and by the 2000 elections, seven out of every ten families were in receipt of food hand-outs of one type or another. With so much at stake, who would dare to vote for opposition candidates?

▼ *A 'fujiloo' in Ayacucho. Carlos Alviar explains: 'Many of the latrines have faults in their construction. They were designed to save materials – but they are so narrow that you almost get stuck inside. Nonetheless, they have led to a decrease in diarrhoeal diseases.'*

Susana Pastor

Susana Pastor

Support from the media, whether purchased by Montesinos or extracted at his behest through blackmail by the tax department or other authorities, was one of the Fujimori regime's major assets. However, not all the media kow-towed to its wishes in this way. Particularly at the local level, many media outlets maintained a critical stance. This was particularly true of local radio stations, like Radio Cutivalú in Piura. Named after Lucas Cutivalú – an indigenous leader who won recognition from imperial Spain when he vigorously defended his ancestral lands in the 16th century – Radio Cutivalú has 200,000 listeners in the Piura region, more than any other station. As well as popular music, the station broadcasts programmes on current affairs, agriculture, and local culture. One of its most popular programmes was a soap opera that focused on the still-contentious issue of land ownership.

Annie Bungeroth

The government employed various methods to deal with media dissent. In the case of Radio Cutivalú, it repeatedly refused applications for an FM broadcasting licence. 'We were trying to get permission since 1996,' says Rodolfo Aquino Ruíz, 'but our application always ended up in the SIN'. The licence was thus never given. With the SIN abolished and Fujimori gone, Radio Cutivalú now has its FM licence. Small-scale, community radio stations like Radio Cutivalú play a key role in providing entertainment, information, and debate, especially to those in isolated rural areas.

Only one winner – how the 2000 elections were rigged

Categorising Fujimori and *fujimorismo* is not easy. By no means a traditional dictator, he was certainly no democrat. Rather, his regime was a hybrid of both elements. As his second term drew on, and as his strategy to win a third term looked increasingly doubtful, its manipulative methods became ever more blatant. This is where Montesinos and the SIN came in. They took the steps required to ensure that Fujimori would win, whatever people's views really were. The judiciary was cajoled into removing the legal obstacles to Fujimori standing. Opposition candidates fell victim to official slur and slander. Television stations were prevailed upon to cover only Fujimori and his campaign, and to ignore the opposition. A clandestine factory was established to turn out millions of fake signatures so that Fujimori's party would be able to demonstrate enough 'support' to register for the elections. And if these efforts were not enough, on the day of the elections the computers were pre-programmed to ensure a Fujimori victory. The fraudulence of the 2000 elections was condemned by an array of international observers.

In the end, Fujimori proved unable to control the situation. In July 2000, tens of thousands of demonstrators filled the streets of Lima to protest at his inauguration for a third term. They came from all over the country, despite the best efforts of the authorities to stop them. The fight for democracy seemed to be reaching a climax. Alejandro Toledo, who had emerged over the previous months as Fujimori's most credible opponent, gained notoriety for leading the demonstrations. The numbers involved revealed the depth of public indignation all over the country. NGOs, grass-roots organisations, and regional pressure groups all played a part. Internationally, the pro-democracy movement was given added impetus by pressure from the USA, Canada, and European countries.

Lacking a democratic tradition

In constructing his authoritarian regime, Fujimori profited from the absence of a strong democratic tradition in Peru. Unlike other Latin American countries – such as Chile, Uruguay, or Costa Rica – Peru cannot look back to a period in its recent history when government really represented the people and their interests. It never developed a strong party system. Peru is accustomed to lengthy periods of authoritarian rule with only restricted popular participation. In the 1920s, the government of Leguía, known as the *oncenio* because Leguía kept office for eleven years (1919-30), was a thinly disguised dictatorship. Leguía has sometimes been compared with Fujimori, not just because he narrowly outdid Fujimori's ten years as president, but because he also opened up the economy to foreign investors, and presided over a period of export-led growth. In the late 1940s and 1950s, Peru was ruled for eight years – the *ochenio* – by General Manuel Odría, a right-winger with a popular touch. From 1968 to 1980, the country was governed by a military dictatorship under first General Juan Velasco (1968-75), and then General Francisco Morales Bermúdez (1975-80). It was under Velasco that the armed forces sought to impose a series of major social and economic reforms.

During these years, there was only one political party that could come close to claiming to represent the mass of the population: APRA. Originally founded in Mexico in 1924 by Víctor Raúl Haya de la Torre, APRA was repeatedly thwarted in its hopes of winning office by democratic means. Hated by Peru's upper class, and feared by the military, the party suffered long periods of repression and clandestinity. It was partly for this reason that it developed as a vertical, top-down political organisation, with little internal democracy. Haya de la Torre, a powerful

LOCAL PROPOSALS FOR CHANGE

Propuesta Regional, in the northern city of Piura, is an example of the sort of local pressure group that developed during the Fujimori regime. It came into being in September 1992, five months after Fujimori's palace coup. It sought to provide a forum for democratic debate following his closure of the regional assemblies. It was backed by a wide range of local institutions, including the Catholic Church, NGOs, media outlets, and an array of civil society organisations.

Annie Bungeroth

Propuesta also sought to bring local interest groups together and to provide an alternative to discredited political parties. It organised discussion and debate, developing activities around three main topics: regional development, decentralisation, and local democracy. Propuesta thus found a way to rally opposition to the government, and to open up a space for change. When democracy was finally restored at the end of 2000, local civic groups found they had a powerful voice with the capacity to influence government in Lima.

orator who had initially been impressed by Italian fascism, drew up a programme of social and political reforms. But he was never able to carry them out. Haya was challenged on the left by the Peruvian Communist Party, although its development was stalled by the premature death in 1930 of its founder and ideologue, José Carlos Mariátegui. The Communist Party's support was concentrated in the union movement, which was never very large given Peru's scant industrialisation. Relations between APRA and the left came under greatest strain during the Cold War of the 1950s when, to gain acceptance, APRA supported Odría and became stridently anti-communist.

The Velasco years were pivotal in many ways. Where APRA had failed to reform Peru 'from below', Velasco and the armed forces sought to do it 'from above'. By nationalising oil and mining operations, Velasco sought to break the power of foreign multinationals. In their place, he created state companies. Through one of Latin America's most ambitious land reform programmes, he tried to break the power of the rural elite and give the land to those who worked on it. By introducing labour participation arrangements in industrial firms, he sought to give workers a share in the profits of their employers. Those previously excluded were thus offered a greater stake in the economy. Backed by force, the military was able to change the traditional power structure. Yet it did so in a high-handed way that overrode the views and aspirations of ordinary people. As it turned out, the so-called 'Revolutionary Government of the Armed Forces' ran into opposition both from those who felt dispossessed, and from those who felt it did not go far enough.

Party politics is a relatively new game in Peru. Although parties existed – APRA and the Communist Party for instance – they did not constitute a 'party system' as such. Following the demise of the military government in 1980, such a system came into being. Political parties competed for office in broadly free and fair elections. The 1980 election was won by *Acción Popular*, a centre-right party whose leader, Fernando Belaunde, had been unceremoniously deposed in 1968 by Velasco. *Acción Popular* governed in alliance with the right-wing *Partido Popular Cristiano* (PPC), a business party. The 1985 elections were won for APRA by Alan García, who tried to reposition his party as a social democratic force. On the left, a myriad of feuding Marxist parties managed to shelve some of their differences and form the United Left coalition, or *Izquierda Unida* (IU). The IU victory in the 1983 Lima municipal elections was the first time that a socialist grouping had ever won democratic control of a capital city in Latin America.

By the end of the 1980s, this incipient party system had collapsed. Beset by the effects of the debt crisis, acute economic instability, hyperinflation, rampant corruption, and by the seemingly unstoppable onslaught of guerrilla violence, Peru's party leaders were found wanting. Belaunde had shown the way: elected in 1980 with 46 per cent of the vote, his party won a mere six per cent in the 1985 elections. The García administration ended in even greater disgrace, even though party loyalty still won APRA 20 per cent of the vote in 1990. Having paraded himself as

▼ *The Congress of the Republic was closed by Fujimori in 1992, and re-opened later that year once new elections had given him a majority. In Peruvian politics, Congress has tended to play a subservient role to the Executive.*

Susana Pastor

the saviour of his country in 1985, García was vilified in 1990 as the author of its virtual collapse. It was in this political vacuum that Peruvians discovered Fujimori, a little-known figure, an outsider to the traditional political class. As the 1990s showed, Fujimori proved to be a canny political player who swiftly realised that his great advantage was his ability to further discredit the mainstream parties and their leaders. Far from creating a public outcry when he violated the constitution in 1992 by closing Congress, he was hailed as a hero who had put the party politicians firmly in their place.

Terror and counter-terror

Few had heard of Sendero Luminoso, or 'Shining Path' as it is known in English, when it took up cudgels against the Peruvian state in 1980. Only those who made a pastime of following the fratricidal feuds and splits in the Peruvian Marxist Left would have known much about Abimael Guzmán, a Kantian philosopher from the University of San Cristóbal de Huamanga in Ayacucho, who had established a small dissident faction from mainstream Maoism back in the late 1960s. By 1990, the names of Sendero Luminoso and Guzmán (or his *nom de guerre*, '*Camarada Gonzalo*') were etched in people's memory everywhere.

Sendero launched its first armed attack on the Peruvian state and its representatives when it tossed a bomb into the polling station at Chuschi,

CAUGHT IN THE CROSSFIRE

Susana Pastor

Huayllay in northern Ayacucho bore more than its fair share of violence during the 1980s, though, unlike other villages in the region, it was never abandoned by its inhabitants. Sendero Luminoso attacked the community on three occasions, murdering 40 people. It would oblige young men and women to join its ranks at gunpoint; if they refused they would be shot. The community mayor, Alejandro Ñaupa Gutiérrez, told us how Sendero had killed his younger brother, and how he himself had narrowly escaped with his life. All families have similar stories to tell. The army also took people away, accusing them of collaborating with Sendero. None were seen again. Many children in Huayllay have grown up as orphans.

an Ayacuchan village, on the occasion of the 1980 presidential elections. Its initial successes were all in the region of Ayacucho, where Sendero had prepared the political ground with care over the preceding years. It took advantage of a sense of frustration and alienation in a region long ignored by Lima, as well as of the ham-fisted response by the authorities to Sendero. Having failed to stem the tide of violence, the Belaunde administration brought in the army at the end of 1982. It mounted a campaign of counter-terror in order to regain support among people in Ayacucho. Massacres and atrocities became commonplace in rural Ayacucho over the years that followed, as Sendero and the military vied for control of territory.

By the mid-1980s, Sendero had opened up new theatres of conflict: in the central highlands of Junín, in the coca-producing Huallaga valley further east, and in the north of the country inland from Trujillo. Most importantly, around 1985, it took the decision to take the Maoist strategy of encircling the towns a stage further by mounting attacks in urban areas, particularly Lima. The development of its links to the drug traffickers of the Huallaga enabled Sendero to buy guns and improve its military capacity. At the same time, another guerrilla grouping, the *Movimiento Revolucionario Túpac Amaru* (MRTA) also took up arms, with its main base in San Martín department in the *selva alta* to the north-east. Influenced more by the Cuban revolution than by Maoism, the MRTA shared neither Sendero's world-view nor its gratuitously violent methods.

Sendero's ability to impose itself on communities stemmed from the terror it instilled among people unable to defend themselves. Where *Sendero* tried to make inroads into places with strong social organisation, it encountered resistance. In the southern department of Puno, for example, with its tightly-knit Aymara-speaking communities, Sendero found it difficult to build support. In the mining communities of the *sierra*, it was also rebuffed. And in Lima, its attempts to infiltrate low-income neighbourhoods met with strong resistance from popular leaders with different ways of thinking and operating.

By the beginning of the 1990s, as Sendero shifted its war to Lima and increased the ferocity of its attacks, it seemed as though the flimsy edifice of the Peruvian state was indeed on the brink of collapse. However, Guzmán's capture in 1992 – a lucky break for the authorities – proved the turning point. Without Guzmán's strong leadership, Sendero lacked the political vision and military capacity to continue as before. What had seemed an irresistible and impenetrable force, rapidly fell apart. A small rump has continued to mount attacks in northern Ayacucho and in the Huallaga valley, but Sendero today is a faint shadow of its former self, restricted to remote areas where its main allies are drug interests. Similarly, the MRTA proved a broken reed. Its last – but perhaps most spectacular – political stunt was the 1997 hostage-taking at the Japanese ambassador's residence in Lima, which led to a three-month-long siege of the building.

► This flour mill in Ayacucho was created to support families displaced by the terror. The women who work here grind flour made of a nutritious combination of nine different Andean grains.

Susana Pastor

▼ Isabel Gutiérrez Palomino is president of the 'mothers' club' at Huayllay. The club brings together single mothers and widows in activities aimed at sustaining and reconstructing the community.

Fujimori's success in dealing with the guerrillas was also a product of a more sophisticated approach to counter-insurgency than the blind violence of the early days. Key to this was the development of community-based local militias, known as *rondas campesinas*, in the early 1980s. The *rondas campesinas* first came into existence in northern Peru, notably in Cajamarca, as peasant communities took steps to defend themselves from cattle rustlers. In Ayacucho, the name was borrowed to describe local militias in which peasants were forced to take part by the army. Still, these new *rondas* responded to real problems of insecurity and fear of attacks by Sendero. As such, they proliferated in the war zone in the early 1990s, but have become less important since.

Susana Pastor

Deepening democracy

Villa El Salvador, a township of some 360,000 inhabitants on Lima's southern rim, is an unusual place: it is a planned city. It first grew out of the sand-dunes in the 1970s, at the time of Velasco's military government. It was a place where the migrant squatters from the *sierra* could settle without fear of being constantly moved on. It grew block by block, on the basis of tight communal organisation. Though born under an authoritarian regime, it soon

THE MURDER OF MARÍA ELENA MOYANO

A turning-point in Sendero Luminoso's attempts to penetrate urban areas was the killing of María Elena Moyano. Moyano was assassinated in Villa El Salvador on February 15 1992, the victim of a Sendero hit squad. First she was shot, then her body was blown to bits with dynamite. A strong community leader and defender of women's rights, María Elena founded *Fepomuves*, the women's federation in Villa El Salvador. She denounced attempts by *senderistas* to sabotage community soup kitchens and other grass-roots organisations. She was killed while inaugurating a new supply centre for the municipality's milk programme for schoolchildren. Her funeral was attended by tens of thousands of people. Her death opened many people's eyes to Sendero's ruthless methods, and its determination to destroy all independent popular organisation. Ten years later, in 2002, Maria Elena Moyano was officially declared a national heroine. Peru's official pantheon of heroes, mostly war leaders and patriots, includes very few women.

▼ *The Creación Sagama shoe workshop is one of the many successful micro-enterprises in Villa El Salvador's industrial park.*

became a symbol of local democracy and self-government. Driven by the strength of civil society in Villa El Salvador, the municipality tried to tackle head-on many of the problems that afflict other low-income neighbourhoods. It created an industrial park, a flourishing area of manufacture and commerce. People from all over Lima come to buy things of recognised quality at competitive prices direct from the producers. The Spanish government conferred upon Villa El Salvador the prestigious Prince of Asturias prize in recognition of its achievements as a community.

While the story of Villa El Salvador is exceptional, it is by no means alone in having a lively civil society. There are thousands of neighbourhood associations and projects all over Lima that provide basic services for the communities they serve. Among the most important are the *comedores populares*, or community kitchens, where food is prepared daily at cost price for members of the community. The experience of working communally has strengthened people's convictions about what can be achieved even in the most adverse conditions. The *comedores* have also opened up a major role for women in community politics that did not previously exist. Community services of different types have frequently been aided by the activities of NGOs and the churches, sources of practical help and financial support. Because of their significance at the local level, especially among women with little previous political experience, the *comedores* have attracted the attentions of political parties. The government, too, sees them as a useful source of grass-roots backing. Under Fujimori, PRONAA, the government agency responsible for food assistance, tried to use the *comedores* to rally support. It threatened to cut off supplies unless the women of the *comedores* agreed to campaign for the ruling party. Despite such pressures, most grass-roots organisations maintained their independence.

Susana Pastor

Building power and influence in civil society

Ilo, a port of some 70,000 people, used to be a company town. Located close to the border with Bolivia and Chile, it was the place where the Southern Peru Copper Corporation (SPCC) shipped out copper from its nearby mines at Toquepala and Cuajone. Despite this, it is a town that has long followed its own agenda, led by a determined left-wing local municipality with close ties to the mineworkers. Supported by *Labor*, an NGO with 18 years' experience in the town, the municipality successfully obliged SPCC to reduce the contamination it causes in Ilo. First, the town won a landmark case in 1991 when it took SPCC to international arbitration at The Hague. The result forced the company to divert the dumping of waste from Toquepala to where it would do less environmental damage. Then SPCC was pressured into a commitment to reduce sulphur dioxide fumes from its smelter in the town. In 1996, the municipality unveiled the town's first strategic plan. Its emphasis is on developing environmental awareness among community leaders, strengthening organisation among communities threatened by mining activities, and working on alternative long-term development policies. As well as programmes to monitor air quality, the strategic plan has led to greater public discussion about municipal spending priorities. In 2002, 40 per cent of the municipal investment budget was allocated by local civil society organisations.

In places less politicised than Ilo, a major limitation faced by community organisations is their restricted ability to influence change at the regional or national level. The collapse of political parties in the 1990s removed from the scene one of the means through which public pressure could influence state policy. Fujimori was able to co-opt popular leaders, or simply ignore their demands. Since Fujimori's departure, this seems to be

▲ *Percy munches bread at the comedor in San Juan de Lurigancho, Lima*

Annie Bungeroth

► *Fumes rise from the refinery at Ilo. Many local people suffer from chronic respiratory problems as a result of poor air quality.*

Susana Pastor

changing, and new institutions, which promise to give greater influence to civil society, are emerging. The negotiations that accompanied the return to democracy in 2000 and 2001 involved grass-roots organisations, NGOs, and church groups in the establishment of special local forums (*mesas de concertación*) to debate and agree new rules and policies.

A central aim of the *mesas* has been to try to close the yawning gap between the state and civil society, made larger by the absence of credible political parties. At the national level, attempts were made to forge a consensus among representative groups from all walks of life. The same model was applied at the regional, and even local, levels. 'This is something completely new,' says Pina Huamán, the president of the *mesa* responsible for metropolitan Lima, 'because the drive behind these is from below, not above.' Under Toledo, a special national *mesa* was established to devise a strategy to combat poverty. Many of the officials who were initially put in charge of the poverty strategy had worked for NGOs previously. They therefore had greater sympathy with grass-roots concerns than some of their predecessors.

▼ *Haydee Moreno Cueza explains some of the problems that women face in taking on leadership roles: 'When I was Vice President of the women's network … I was a lot more involved, and my husband really didn't like it. He used to say, "Why are you going out so much, why do you have so many meetings?" I'd say, "You've got your work, they give you training….And when we have meetings, I tell you what the meetings are about, I show you leaflets." But he didn't like that, he'd go off and come back drunk, and start throwing things and banging the table.'*

Annie Bungeroth

The work of the *mesas* has further enhanced the role of women in public life. Women have traditionally tended to assume a subordinate role in politics, with limited presence in Congress and in government. This appears to be changing. Reforms to the electoral laws say that at least one-third of party lists for Congress must be made up of women, although of those finally elected to Congress in 2001, only 20 per cent were women. Feminist pressure groups like *Flora Tristán* believe that a lot more has to change before women can really play their role to the maximum. Women will have to extricate themselves from unpaid domestic responsibilities. 'The state needs to provide such facilities as crèches that allow women to become citizens,' says Flora Tristán's María Emma Manarelli. She argues that the lack of such facilities is one reason why so few women from lower-income groups can engage in politics, while this is easier for those from middle- or upper-class backgrounds, who usually have help at home.

Susana Pastor

▲ *Rosa Rivero is the president of CEPRODA MINGA, an NGO, based in Piura, which works with rural communities to develop local plans for sustainable development.*

Increasing decentralisation

Decentralisation is an important way of increasing people's involvement in governmental decision-making, and of bridging the gap between society and the state. Reflecting its authoritarian tradition, and the dominance of its capital, Peru has always been a highly centralised country. Almost all decisions are made in Lima, and local government has little real power. It depends almost entirely on the centre for funding, and receives less than four per cent of the national budget. With government under Fujimori more centralised than ever, one of the main demands of the opposition was to win a new deal for the regions. President Toledo has promised to raise local government spending to 15 per cent of the budget by 2006, and to create new regional authorities. Real devolution, however, implies giving local government the resources to fund its own programmes, while ensuring that these are open, participatory, and transparent. Yet it remains to be seen to what extent Toledo is genuinely determined and able to devolve fiscal responsibility to the regions.

Another aspect of decentralisation involves local people in planning their future. In spite of everything, some timid steps were taken in this direction under Fujimori. In Ayacucho, for instance, local NGOs were invited to work with local communities in a scheme to prioritise community needs and to give them a bigger say in how development funds were spent. Although the plan was half-hearted, and was never followed through, the experience set an important precedent. The ability of local communities to undertake such schemes depends greatly on the vision of local authorities, particularly mayors. Where such local leadership exists, important advances can be made. The town of Limatambo in Cuzco is an example. At the behest of its mayor, in 1993 the municipality embarked on an experiment in popular participation that became an object lesson to mayors elsewhere. Opening the accounts of the municipality to regular public scrutiny, for instance, has helped to generate poular confidence in local leaders. Participation has also led to the surrounding peasant communities having a more direct role in decision-making. In Piura, too, led on by Propuesta Regional, there were important steps in this direction. These experiences suggest that economic transparency is the key condition for participatory planning.

Peru's beleaguered economy

The lure of the mines

As in the colonial past, Peru's economic future is once again pinned on mining. When fully developed, the huge Antamina mine in Ancash will be Peru's single most important source of foreign exchange. Situated in the Callejón de Conchucos, Antamina is the country's largest single investment project, and will become one of the world's biggest copper and zinc mines. It is owned by a conglomerate of Canadian, British, and Australian companies. It represents an investment of 2.3 billion dollars, and should add 900 million dollars to Peru's annual export earnings. Antamina follows on the heels of Yanacocha in Cajamarca, owned jointly by Buenaventura of Peru and Newmont Mining of the USA. Yanacocha is Latin America's largest gold mine, and among the world's most profitable. Other international companies are also investing in Peru's resource wealth, taking advantage of the incentives offered to foreign investors by Fujimori. In the energy sector, for instance, foreign companies are pushing ahead with the development of the giant Camisea gas reserves in the jungle to the north of Cuzco.

These projects should raise Peru's export potential substantially over the next ten years, with investment from abroad helping to satisfy its appetite for capital. However, heavier dependence on mining will increase

▶ *Santa Claus and his reindeer touch down at the Southern Peru (SPCC) mine at Toquepala. SPCC managed to avoid being nationalised during the 1970s, and it is now owned by a Mexican-based company.*

Susana Pastor

Peru's vulnerability to fluctuations on the notoriously unstable world metals markets, while in the longer term, profit remittances from Peru to the investing countries may outweigh any new investment. Typically, mining tends to bring little by way of development to the areas where mines are located. There are few linkages into other sectors of the local economy, and modern mining produces few jobs. Many of the mine's needs – including even food for the miners – are imported from abroad. Mining thus creates a much more uneven pattern of growth than, say, agriculture, which generates many more employment spin-offs. And, as we shall see later, mining often brings environmental problems and conflicts with local communities.

From the time of the *conquistadores* onwards, Peru's integration into the world economy has primarily been through its mines. Yet, a century ago, the country had a more diversified range of exports than most in Latin America, reflecting its varied geography and rich endowment of natural resources. Copper mining, concentrated in the central *sierra* in and around Cerro de Pasco, accounted for just over 20 per cent of exports on the eve of the First World War. In the 19th and early 20th centuries, the country experienced short-term booms in other commodities, notably *guano* (seabird droppings, used as a fertiliser) and rubber. Sugar exports represented 15.4 per cent of exports in 1914.

Peru began to promote a manufacturing base in the 1960s and 1970s, rather later than other large Latin American countries. The Velasco government copied the model, employed elsewhere in Latin America, of encouraging 'import-substituting industrialisation' as a way of developing a more balanced economy, and reducing dependence on a handful of export commodities. Protected by high tariffs, Peruvian manufacturers were able to supply local markets without fear of competition from cheap imports. As a consequence, the numbers of firms and people employed in manufacturing increased substantially in these years. At the same time, the state sector took over control of key export industries, principally mining and petroleum, from US-owned multinationals. Thus, the Cerro de Pasco Corporation became Centromin, and the International Petroleum Corporation (IPC) became Petroperú.

Since Velasco, and under international pressure from organisations like the IMF and the World Bank, Peru has been forced to modify this model of state-led development in favour of a more liberal approach, abandoning import substitution for a return to the more traditional model of 'export-led growth'. Privatisation of state companies began under Belaunde (1980-85), but was pursued with much greater vigour under Fujimori (1990-2000). The legislation on foreign investment was revised to make it more attractive to foreign investors, as were tax laws. Controls on capital movements and profit repatriation were eased, and barriers to imports were dismantled. The new model, it was hoped, would generate the export-led growth required for Peru to service its burgeoning foreign debt.

The burden of debt

One of the main deficiencies of the Velasco model was its failure to hit on sustainable ways of financing development. Bereft of foreign investment, and lacking a self-confident private sector or local capital market, the state became the motor for development. Without a tax system to fund expanded state activities, the Velasco government began to borrow from abroad. At the same time, the international banking system was awash with recycled 'petrodollars' after the 1972 OPEC decision to increase oil prices. Banks were under great pressure to use this glut of money to increase lending. World interest rates were low, and commodity prices generally high. Bankers fell over themselves to offer loans on attractive terms, especially to oil exporters like Peru, with little thought as to the possible longer-term consequences. For their part, the Peruvian authorities, strapped for cash, seized the opportunity. With prices in dollars rising faster than world interest rates (thus reducing the value of debt in real terms), it made a great deal of sense to be a borrower.

Consequently, Peru's foreign debt – like that of many other Latin American countries in these years – ballooned. It increased sevenfold between 1970-79. The increased burden of repaying the debt and the interest due on it rose as a result. In fact, the debt crisis in Peru began in 1975, seven years before Mexico announced in 1982 that it could no longer afford to honour its debts, triggering a crisis across Latin America. As dollar interest rates began to climb once again in the late 1970s, and commodity prices fell, the attractions of being a borrower diminished. Initially saved from default by the inauguration of the SPCC Cuajone copper mine in Moquegua, the *coup de grâce* for Peru came in 1982 when Mexico defaulted on its repayments. Horrified, international bankers cut off all new lending to Latin America. Peru struggled on for two years, unable to borrow new money to pay off old debts, before finally defaulting in 1984.

▼ *This* arpillera, *or wall-hanging, was sewn by women from Manuela Ramos, a Peruvian NGO. It shows Peru's debt rising as sacks of dollars make their way towards the USA and Europe. While politicians make promises on TV, and the rich dream of Miami, shopping bags are empty, schools and hospitals crumble, and a demonstration demanding higher wages is met by a tank.*

SUCCESSFUL SMALL EXPORTERS

Not all exporters are multinationals or state concerns. In some areas, with a bit of help, small-scale producers have been able to sell to foreign markets. In Piura, as elsewhere in Peru, coffee is mostly grown on very small-scale, poor family farms, farming only 1-2 hectares of land apiece. With the assistance of CEPICAFE, a producers' association that defends the interests of growers and provides them with services, coffee growers in Piura have been able to access the export market, bypassing the traditional export houses. They have been able to take advantage of premium markets for organic and fair trade coffee. CEPICAFE has helped producers replant with better quality coffee, providing them with necessary technical assistance. It has raised the incomes of member farmers substantially, encouraging increasing numbers to do likewise. Other similar organisations are working in other coffee-producing areas of the country.

▲ *Coffee seedlings, Piura*

▼ *CEPICAFE growers meet at Pite, in Piura.*

Susana Pastor

FAIR TRADE – A BETTER DEAL FOR POOR FARMERS

Fair trade schemes offer Peruvian coffee farmers a 'floor' price for their coffee, of $125 per 100 lbs (or *quintal*). Not only is this much higher than the world price – which stood at a 30-year low of $45 per *quintal* at the end of 2001 – but it provides farmers with a guarantee against price fluctuations, the bane of most small-scale commodity producers. Consumers in developed countries pay a small premium for the fairly-traded coffee they buy, but most of the difference in the prices paid to farmers is a result of the elimination of intermediaries. It is these, especially the roasters, who gain most in times of depressed prices. In 2001, fair trade coffee accounted for barely two per cent of exports. Though this proportion is set to rise significantly, fair trade is unlikely to become much more than a specialist niche in the near future.

The debt crisis in Peru was made worse by the poor use to which much of the money had been put. Untrammelled, military spending increased rapidly in the 1970s. Justified at the time by the supposed threat of aggression from Pinochet's Chile, arms spending rose unchecked, and much of this money was wasted through institutional corruption. Pharaonic development projects, such as the Majes project in Arequipa, were based on doubtful cost-benefit calculations. Typically, they cost considerably more than planned, with the main beneficiaries of this over-spending being the foreign construction firms involved. Peruvian exports, stagnant for much of the 1980s, failed completely to keep up with ever-rising debt service requirements.

In 1985, Peru shocked the financial world by announcing that henceforth it would pay no more than ten per cent of the value of its annual exports on debt servicing. Newly-elected on a wave of public hostility to the IMF and its economic policies, President Alan García decided to confront the international financial community. Although Peru had already entered into default on some of its international loans the previous year, the burden of debt had become unsustainable. García's stance was not as uncompromising as it seemed, however; in the years that followed, Peru paid considerably more than ten per cent. But his up-front position angered international bankers, and they sought to punish Peru, making it an example to the rest of the world of the costs of defiance.

After 1990, under Fujimori, a penitent Peru returned to the international fold, promising to make every effort to repay the debt and to toe the IMF line in future. The hyperinflation and recession of García's last two years in office were a bad advertisement for the case for confrontation. In return for Fujimori's compliance with their policy preferences, the IMF and World Bank agreed to a debt renegotiation. Eventually, Peru was also able to renegotiate debts to foreign governments and the commercial banks. Fujimori made prompt debt repayment one of the unwavering principles of his administration, aware that his social programmes depended on flows of cash from the World Bank and the Inter-American Development Bank (IDB). Debt-servicing continued to absorb a large proportion of government spending, forcing spending cuts in other areas. Meanwhile, Peru continued to contract new loans to pay off the old. At the end of 2000, the total foreign debt stood at $28.3 billion (the equivalent of 50.5 per cent of GDP, the total value of all goods and services). When Fujimori came to office ten years before, the figure had been $22.8 billion.

UNETHICAL DEBT

In order to draw public attention to the corrupt use of debt, in January 2000, in Quito, NGOs from all the Andean countries decided to set up the Andean Debt Tribunal. The Tribunal defined corruptly-used debt as 'illegitimate' and stated that as such, it should not be repaid. Much of the Andean debt had been used for non-productive purposes, such as arms purchases. The Tribunal thus sought to scrutinise debt from an ethical point of view, not just an economic one. Exemplary cases were selected to show how debts had been contracted simply to further private interests, with little or no public benefit. The Peruvian case chosen was the use of loans in 1983 to buy two ships from Italy for the then state-owned shipping company (CPV). These broke down on their maiden voyage and could never be used again. This single example cost the public purse $90 million.

The role of the Tribunal was given added force when, in August 2001, the Peruvian Congress agreed to set up a commission to look into the uses and abuses of Peruvian debt. Senior public officials under Fujimori were suspected of having used their positions to make money out of the conversion of commercial debt into Brady bonds in 1997. While the formation of the Tribunal has been welcomed as a positive initiative, the work involved in tracing the corrupt use of public debt is still at a preliminary stage.

Total debt-servicing cost the country the equivalent of 45.4 per cent of annual exports in 2000, and absorbed 39 per cent of all government spending that year.

To bolster his reputation in international financial circles, Fujimori sought to avoid any hint that Peru might seek to negotiate some sort of debt reduction. He spurned the activities of the Jubilee 2000 campaign which, backed by the Catholic Church and millions of Peruvians, argued the case for debt relief. As a medium-sized debtor country, Peru was ineligible for debt reduction under the Highly Indebted Poor Country (HIPC) scheme, backed by the World Bank. The World Bank is reluctant to extend debt relief to larger debtor countries, even when, like Peru, they are arguably both 'highly indebted' and 'poor'.

Fujieconomics: structural adjustment and economic liberalisation

Prodded on by the IMF, most countries in Latin America embarked on economic liberalisation, or 'structural adjustment' as it is known, in the 1980s or 1990s. Few went down this road with greater speed or zeal than Peru under Fujimori. The retreat from the state-centred development model had begun timidly in the early 1980s under Belaunde, only to be reversed by Alan García. The return to orthodoxy began with a vengeance with the so-called 'Fujishock' of August 1990, a massive price adjustment which sought to stabilise inflation. In the months that lay ahead, other policy changes followed thick and fast. The main architect of this transformation was Carlos Boloña, Fujimori's finance minister after 1991. Boloña, most agree, was more of a *fondomonetarista* (an enthusiastic apologist for the IMF and its policies) than the IMF itself.

At the core of policy was the belief that state intervention should be pared back to the minimum, and that the private sector should drive the economy. Prices, in particular, should be determined by unfettered market forces, not by state intervention. This *laissez-faire* philosophy harked back to the liberalism of the past, and for this reason was labelled 'neo-liberalism'. Neo-liberal policies included the sale of most of Peru's state companies, or their closure where no-one wanted to buy them. Between 1990-95, the majority of public companies – including interests in mines,

banking, telecommunications, electricity providers, and other utilities – were privatised. Structural adjustment also involved a radical overhaul of those activities that remained in state hands. In some cases, such as the tax office (SUNAT), the old structures were simply closed down and replaced by new ones.

Insofar as the outside world was concerned, structural adjustment involved adopting policies to encourage free trade and to attract foreign investment. The basic idea was to promote export growth and inward investment, generating foreign exchange to make it easier to service the foreign debt. To this end, Peru sharply reduced the tariffs it imposed on imports, and removed all other non-tariff barriers like prohibitions and quotas. In 1990, tariffs averaged 56 per cent; the following year they were lowered to two basic rates of 15 per cent and 25 per cent. By 1996 they had dropped to levels well below those of other Andean countries. The effects of trade liberalisation were enhanced by the government's exchange rate policy. After a large initial devaluation in 1990, the Peruvian *sol* appreciated against the US dollar for much of the 1990s, exposing local producers to ever greater foreign competition. The government's aim was to prevent any resurgence of inflation and make business more internationally competitive.

Susana Pastor

▲ Over the last decade, Lima has seen an invasion of casinos, the result of liberalisation of the gaming laws under Fujimori. Slot machines are a lure for those desperate to win a quick buck; but the casinos are the real winners.

Fujimori's economic policies were successful in eliminating inflation. This peaked in 1990 at a staggering 7650 per cent, but fell swiftly in the years that followed. In 2001, prices rose by only 3.7 per cent. Although the Fujishock hit people hard in the short-term, the slowdown in inflation brought relief longer-term, especially to people on lower incomes whose meagre earnings had been whittled away in real terms by rampant inflation. From 1993-97, Fujimori was also successful in restoring economic growth. Nevertheless, this represented only a partial recovery from the downturn of the late 1980s. GDP per head of the population in 1997 was still well below its rate of ten years earlier. Within the international financial community, Fujimori's 'success' was enthusiastically interpreted as a vindication of neoliberal economics, and a cautionary tale for other governments that might be tempted to confront their creditors or abandon IMF-backed orthodoxy.

JUBILEE 2000 – A GLOBAL MOVEMENT TO END DEBT

In 1999, within a space of two months, two million Peruvians signed a petition demanding debt relief for the country. The petition was supported by the Catholic Church, whose Bishops' Conference took the lead locally in spearheading the international Jubilee 2000 campaign. According to Laura Vargas of the Church's Social Action office (CEAS), the topic of debt had been 'taboo' since Alan García's time. She claims that the campaign turned debt 'from an issue for economists into an issue for housewives', adding that, 'It was much more successful than we had ever imagined, with everyone supporting it apart from the banks and the government.' CEAS calculates that $16 billion left Peru in debt-servicing between 1990 and 2000, while new debt totalled $13 billion (of which most went on repaying old debts). The value of the campaign lay mainly in raising awareness and getting large numbers of people involved. 'It encouraged us to be part of a global movement,' says Vargas, 'and to be able to question the way the world works.' Fujimori ignored the Jubilee petition and its recommendations, but Toledo said that he would seek to renegotiate Peru's debts. Twelve months into his five-year term, however, there were few signs of this happening.

In other respects, 'Fujieconomics' were less of a resounding success. Although Peru's exports increased, they were hardly an advertisement for 'export-led growth'. They stood at just over $6 billion at the end of the 1990s, only twice their level 20 years earlier. Exports in other countries, such as Colombia and Chile, had increased much faster. Incomes recovered some of their purchasing power as inflation slowed, but in the late 1990s they remained depressed: salaries for white-collar workers in greater Lima rose slightly in real terms, while wages for blue-collar workers slumped.

Susana Pastor

▲ Workers made redundant from the judiciary are on hunger strike in front of the Palace of Justice. They demand reposición – re-instatement in their jobs.

▼ Money changers sporting dollar signs are a frequent sight in Lima. Most wealthy Peruvians prefer to keep their money in dollars.

Susana Pastor

The neo-liberal recipe was found most wanting in the area of job creation. Even in the 1980s, the labour market was characterised by a large 'informal sector', with people working long hours in precarious conditions without employment contracts, access to collective bargaining, or social security entitlements. With the economic collapse of the late 1980s, the numbers working in the informal sector grew swiftly. This was particularly the case for women, whose involvement in the informal sector is reckoned to have increased from 37 per cent in 1984 to 52 per cent in 1993.

The renewal of growth in the 1990s did not bring with it an increase in formal sector employment. Instead, the closure of manufacturing plants under the weight of cheap imports, and job losses as a result of privatisation and rationalisation, turned the job market into one of cut-throat competition between those looking for work. According to Juan Carlos Vargas from PLADES, an NGO that provides advice to trade unions, as many as 750,000 public sector workers lost their jobs during the 1990s. Dismissals were made easier as a result of changes to the labour code that reduced workers' rights. Often among the first to go were 'troublesome' union organisers. Labour reforms under Fujimori removed some of the limits on working hours, and reduced employees' rights to claim indemnities for dismissal.

Patterns of employment were changing in other ways. In service industries in particular, women tended to replace male employees. Many employers chose to hire female workers because they believed them to be less likely to form unions, and because they could pay them lower wages. At the same time, labour reforms meant that women lost the right to claim maternity leave or to refuse to work at nights, on Sundays, and on public holidays. The 1993 constitution removed the principle – never heeded in practice – of equal pay for men and women.

It is difficult to establish with any precision the number of Peruvians who enjoy full employment rights. The official labour ministry figures suggest that those 'adequately employed' represented just under half of the workforce in 2000. But according to Carmen Vildoso, the vice-minister of labour, the informal sector – defined as 'unqualified independent labourers' – represented 60 per cent of the workforce at the end of 2001.

BUILDING A FAMILY BUSINESS

Raúl Villegas and Marta Oré make underwear on the roof of their house in the San Fernando neighbourhood of San Juan de Lurigancho in Lima. They live close to the point where the valley sides become so steep that not even the poorest family can perch a house there. They started three years ago. At the beginning, they would make goods three days a week, and then spend the rest of the time trying to sell them. When we visited, the whole family was at work. A consignment of bright yellow men's briefs was being readied for dispatch to Bagua and Jaén in the north of Peru. As well as relying on their own dynamism to sell their wares, Raúl and Marta are part of a network of contacts through the local evangelical church community. 'We had no experience at all at the beginning,' Raúl says, 'and we made lots of mistakes.' Over the last two years they have doubled their output, even though prices have fallen. Raúl and Marta have received working capital and business advice from INPET, an NGO working in San Juan.

To stimulate informal employment, the Toledo administration unveiled its *A Trabajar* ('To Work') programme at the end of 2001, promising to provide temporary employment to 270,000 workers (in both urban and rural areas) over two years. It remains to be seen how successful *A Trabajar* will be. A similar make-work programme introduced by García took people off the streets, but failed to increase their skills or improve their chances in the job market. When the scheme ended, those 'employed' returned to the streets. Moreover, the scheme became a thinly-veiled mechanism for building support for the then ruling APRA party among the urban poor.

The Fujimori years also failed to make much impact on poverty, despite the fact that the Fujimori government spent large sums of money on poverty relief. Figures from official household surveys between 1985-2000 suggest that 54 per cent of the population were living in poverty (under a poverty line equivalent to roughly $2 a day) in 2000, compared with 41.6 per cent in 1985. Poverty rates increased greatly at the end of the 1980s, largely because of hyperinflation. In 1991, the rate was 57.4 per cent, falling to 50.7 per cent in 1997, but rising once again in the last three years of the decade. In 1985, 18.4 per cent of the population lived in extreme poverty (earning less than $1 a day), increasing to 26.8 per cent in 1991, but falling back to 24.4 per cent in 2001. Though the best available, these figures should be taken with a pinch of salt. Measuring income is not necessarily the best way of gauging poverty, especially in a country where many people are subsistence farmers. Moreover, a study conducted by the National Statistics Institute in 2001 (after Fujimori's fall) suggested that earlier poverty figures had been deliberately massaged by the authorities to give a positive spin to government policy.

The fall in levels of extreme poverty at the end of the 1990s reflects the impact of the Fujimori government's food assistance and temporary work programmes. When he launched the government's four-year Targeted Strategy to Fight Extreme Poverty (1996-2000), Fujimori promised to halve the number of people living in extreme poverty over this period. The strategy involved building schools and health posts in rural areas, building roads and irrigation systems, and providing food assistance and birth control facilities. It was criticised for failing to help poor farmers produce more, or market their crops better, and there was widespread concern that once the government spending stopped, people would be no better off. Social spending in rural areas had a clear political purpose. The dramatic increase in spending prior to his 1995 presidential victory brought Fujimori immediate political dividends. Also, in the build-up to the 2000 elections, many people complained bitterly that state officials threatened to suspend assistance unless voters came out openly to support Fujimori's second re-election campaign. As we have seen, seven out of every ten Peruvian families were in receipt of food aid of one sort or another at the time of the 2000 elections.

COMEDORES: CATERING FOR THE COMMUNITY

There are some 3500 *comedores* (community kitchens) in Lima, providing cheap food to communities where people could not otherwise afford to eat enough. There are also *comedores* in many other cities. They cater for community members on the lowest incomes. The vast majority of the workers in the *comedores* are women. They do not receive payment, although they and their families can eat for free. The *comedores* work on a shoestring budget. They receive donations of basic foods, usually rice, beans, and cooking oil, from PRONAA, the government food aid agency. The rest they buy themselves in the local market each day, though some buy direct from producers as far away as Huancayo, high in the Andes. The day we visited the *Cinco de Mayo* ('Fifth of May') *comedor* in Pamplona Alta in southern Lima, the menu consisted of corn-mash soup, mashed potato, and meat stew. Anita Teves Quispe, that day's cook, was expecting to feed 120 people at lunchtime. There are five other *comedores* in the district, each providing lunches six days a week. A meal costs a *sol* (20 pence), but is usually given free to schoolchildren and the elderly. 'We have to strike a balance between quality and people's ability to pay,' says Anita.

Rapid increase in the number of *comedores* took place in the late 1980s as rapid inflation eroded people's incomes. In many districts, they became the main defence against widespread hunger in poor neighbourhoods. Since then, they have become a permanent feature of urban life. For many women, working in a *comedor* is a stepping stone to participation in other kinds of community organisation. Some of the women we spoke to work in the *comedor* in the morning, and attend training sessions in the afternoon, where they learn other new skills.

Growing inequalities

The impact of economic liberalisation on inequality is even harder to measure than its impact on poverty. However, studies suggest that inequality became more marked during the 1990s, because the benefits of resumed growth in the economy were very unequally shared. One economic measure of inequality is the 'Gini coefficient'. The nearer the coefficient is towards 100, the greater the degree of inequality in a given population. According to *Cuanto*, a private firm that gathers statistics, the Peruvian Gini coefficient for 1999 was 46.2. In 1994 it had been 44.9. A coefficient of 46.2 is a high figure, placing Peru roughly on a par with Kenya or Madagascar in Africa. This increase in inequality is due less to the fact that the poor became poorer, but that the wealthiest sectors flourished. Economic liberalisation, especially privatisation, generated lucrative business opportunities for a few. The growth in the number of luxury homes in districts like Monterico is indicative of this. Meanwhile,

Susana Pastor

► Subsistence farmers in Huayllay take part in a faena, or communal work party. Community members aged from eight to 60 work together to plough and sow the communal fields.

a tax system weighted heavily towards taxes on consumption rather than on income or profit, means that there is little redistribution of this wealth. The wealthiest sectors of Peruvian society are adept at avoiding tax payment, even though steps were taken by Fujimori to tighten up on tax evasion. One of the worst-hit sectors was the middle class. Always fairly small in Peru, its living standards fell because of the decline in public sector employment, and the contraction of domestic industry.

Liberalisation and agriculture

Agriculture provides a fragile living for a large proportion of Peru's poor. The vast majority of farmers have little land, and no permanent access to water. Many remain largely or wholly subsistence farmers, although those reliant on selling agricultural goods to urban markets have increased greatly in recent decades. The productivity of agriculture varies a great deal from one part of the country to another. It is much higher in the irrigated valleys of the coast than in the highlands. For example, in Puno in the *sierra*, the average yield for potatoes is six tonnes per hectare; in Ica, on the coast, a hectare produces as much as 45 tonnes. Agricultural production is volatile for two key reasons. The first is climatic. Peru's exposure to the *El Niño* weather phenomenon has a direct – and sometimes dramatic – impact on agriculture, upsetting normal rainfall patterns and causing flooding or drought. The second reason is variation in demand for food. Since 1970, Peru has undergone extremes of macroeconomic volatility with periodic downturns in people's living standards. As incomes fall, especially among the poor, demand for food slumps, and agricultural prices decline.

THE POTATO

The potato, it is sometimes said, is Peru's single most important contribution to world agriculture. The Spanish *conquistadores* first brought the potato to Europe at the end of the 16th century as a botanical curiosity. By the 19th century, it had become one of Europe's major staples, and today, global annual potato production is around 300 million tonnes. Peruvians have been growing potatoes for at least 8000 years, and the potato is still the most important crop for the Andean peasant producer. Reputedly, there are some 3800 varieties available, more than in any other country in the world. Peru is also the original home of the sweet potato, and a variety of tubers and roots.

The potato has great nutritional value, and a single medium-sized potato contains about a half an adult's daily requirement of vitamin C, as well as more proteins and calcium than other staples. Yet in Peru, it forms an increasingly small part of most people's diet. It is being displaced by wheat and rice, much of which is imported. Even some potatoes are now imported, for instance those used for chips in fast-food outlets.

It is difficult to disentangle the effects of economic liberalisation from these other factors, but it is clear that trade liberalisation – in conjunction with the overvalued currency – had a marked effect on agricultural prices in the 1990s. This is not so much because agricultural exports increased, but because imports rose steeply, undercutting Peruvian farmers. With imports now accounting for just under half of all food needs, Peruvian agriculture is faced with an ever-decreasing domestic demand for food. Peruvian agriculture produced 200 kg of food per head of the population in the early 1970s, but only 130 kg by the late 1990s.

Agricultural prices experienced a dramatic fall in real terms as a result of the economic difficulties of the late 1980s. Low prices hit all farmers, although those producing mainly for export were less affected. During the 1990s, prices remained depressed even though growth rates in the economy improved. One of the reasons for this was the influx of cheap food from abroad, particularly from North America, which forced local producers to lower their prices. During the 1990s, Peru resorted to importing food products (such as rice, maize, and even potatoes) in which it is a major producer. At the same time, the liberalisation of food imports has accelerated changes in patterns of consumption. For example, the import of wheat flour (for which all protection was removed in 1998) has helped increase consumption of bread and pasta, at the expense of traditional Andean grains. Even in the *sierra*, consumption of highly nutritious indigenous grains – like quinua or kiwicha – is fast declining as consumers switch to imported alternatives. This is not just a matter of price, but of changes in consumer preferences and perceptions: eating bread and pasta is associated with 'being urban'. To return to eating quinua is seen as a step backwards by many recent migrants to the city.

The withdrawal of the state from agriculture is another impact of economic liberalisation felt by Peruvian farmers. In 1991, the Fujimori government closed down the *Banco Agrario* – the state-run rural bank – as part of its policy to wind up state development banks of all sorts. Although the *Banco Agrario* had been corruptly managed, and had never lent to the poorest *campesinos*, its closure removed the only source of credit available to many medium-sized farmers. Commercial banks, the government thought, would fill the hole left by the demise of *Banco Agrario*. In fact, the commercial banks refused to lend to farmers, or offered loans at interest rates that most could not afford.

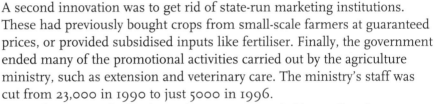

▶ *Fresh bread comes out of the oven at one of the bakeries in San Juan de Lurigancho. The bakeries were started by groups of women involved in the local comedores. The women received training from CIDIAG, a local NGO, to learn how to market and sell the bread they make.*

Annie Bungeroth

▼ *Esperanza del Aguila lives in Rioja, on the edge of the jungle. She prepares palm leaves for making* sombreros *– Latin American-style straw hats. The leaves have been boiling overnight, and Esperanza must spend the morning beating them against a tree to soften them. After a day's drying, she'll send them to the town of Celendín to be made into hats.*

Susana Pastor

A second innovation was to get rid of state-run marketing institutions. These had previously bought crops from small-scale farmers at guaranteed prices, or provided subsidised inputs like fertiliser. Finally, the government ended many of the promotional activities carried out by the agriculture ministry, such as extension and veterinary care. The ministry's staff was cut from 23,000 in 1990 to just 5000 in 1996.

Those worst hit by these changes were probably small-scale producers selling direct into the urban market. The dismantling of the coastal co-operatives, originally created by the 1970s agrarian reform, and the division of the land into small individual plots, greatly expanded the numbers of small-scale farmers. During the course of the 1990s, thousands went bankrupt, turning either to other rural activities (like producing handicrafts), or migrating to the cities.

Not all agriculture suffered, however. Those who were able to identify export markets and weather the volatility of international agricultural commodity markets, could do well. One particular boom industry – at least for a while – was asparagus. Peruvian entrepreneurs struck on a niche export market for a product that had never previously been grown in the country. In large areas of the coast, especially in Ica, to the south of Lima, traditional crops like cotton were uprooted and the land replanted with asparagus. In the case of asparagus, the commercial banks were prepared to lend substantial amounts for what looked like a sure-fire success story. Armies of labourers were employed (mostly women) to harvest the crop, usually at very low wages and with meagre working and living conditions. However, like other boom commodities in the past, the asparagus 'bubble' burst.

► Juan Silupu Rivas runs a small carob-processing factory in Locuto, Tambo Grande. The plant produces a range of products derived from carob trees, including honey and carob powder. Its future is placed at risk by the development of mining in Tambo Grande.

Susana Pastor

The industry suffered from over-production, and intense competition from lower-cost rivals like China. The collapse in asparagus prices in the late 1990s brought in its wake bankruptcies and bad debts for the banks.

In other sectors, too, producers were able to open up export opportunities. The fruit growers of the San Lorenzo valley of Piura grow lemons and mangoes which have established a good reputation in the USA and Europe. The farmers in the valley are smallholders who bought land in the 1960s, taking advantage of a World Bank irrigation scheme. Peruvian coffee producers – almost all of whom are small-scale farmers – have also been able to seize export opportunities. However, at the end of the 1990s, many were hit by the collapse of prices in the international coffee market.

Coca and the drug economy

Minerals apart, Peru once had the dubious distinction of inserting itself into the world economy as the largest purveyor of coca, the raw material for cocaine. In response to the huge increase in the use of cocaine in the 1980s in North America, Europe, and other parts of the developed world, production of coca in Peru flourished. Between 1980-86, the total area planted with coca rose from 10,000 to nearly 200,000 hectares. Soaring coca prices made this the crop of choice for many thousands of poor peasant farmers who had moved to the *selva* to escape the political violence and grinding poverty of the *sierra*. At its height, coca provided a living for 50,000 families.

Coca leaves have been cultivated for thousands of years in Peru and Bolivia. Traditionally, rural labourers chew them to stave off the effects of cold, fatigue, and hunger. The coca leaf has a very special place in Andean

COFFEE DIVIDENDS

Matilde Huamán lives with her husband Alejandro and eight children in La Capilla, a coffee-growing hamlet near Canchaque in Piura. Many of the producers in La Capilla have organised themselves in recent years, with the help of CEPICAFE. At least half of the members of the local coffee growers' association are women. Matilde recounts how she has been using new techniques to improve the quality of her coffee, which she sells to CEPICAFE for export. 'We've all learnt how to prune our coffee plants and get a better harvest. My husband has started germinating coffee and planting seedlings. These are already starting to bear fruit. I have been able to feed my family better. We grow our coffee and give it to CEPICAFE and they sell it for us. When we deliver our coffee, CEPICAFE gives us some money to tide us over. After the harvest, we get a guaranteed price per *quintal* [46 kilos]. Before, we used to sell to private traders for any price we could get. We'd get 120 *soles* per *quintal*. CEPICAFE pays 180 *soles*, and this year it will be more, about 220 *soles*.'

folklore and traditional religious beliefs. Visitors arriving at high altitudes also benefit from infusions made of coca, one of the best palliatives for *soroche*, or altitude sickness. Traditionally, most Peruvian coca was grown in the valleys of La Convención and Lares, areas of *selva alta* in the Cuzco region. However, the new coca plantations (*cocales*) of the 1980s took root further north, mainly in the valley of the River Huallaga. The town of Tingo María, in Huánuco, became the Peruvian coca capital, with *cocales* spreading far and wide down-river into the vicinities of remote and lawless towns like Aucayacu, Uchiza, and Tocache. This was already drug country when Sendero Luminoso began to operate in the area in the mid-1980s, acting as defender of the coca growers (*cocaleros*), and receiving a pay-off in return. Visitors went to Tocache at their peril; several investigative journalists went there at that time, and never came back.

▼ *Women chew coca leaves as they rest.*

For poor peasants, coca has much to recommend it. It commands a high price in the market, usually much higher than other crops. It is a hardy species that copes well with climatic variation. Best of all, it can be harvested four or five times during the year, so that it provides the growers with a steady stream of income. However, being involved in the coca business has its drawbacks. The relationship between powerful coca purchasers and the small-scale *cocaleros* is often highly exploitative, in addition to which, clandestine coca trafficking activities are associated with violence, variously perpetrated by traffickers (*narcos*), by Sendero, and by the state itself. As well as violence, the coca economy encourages drinking, prostitution, and – of course – drug consumption in the growing areas. It has disrupted traditional patterns of peasant family life, and generated a new climate of insecurity. As part of the US administration's 'war on drugs', it has become the target for eradication programmes, spearheaded in the Alto Huallaga and other coca-growing zones by USAID.

By the mid-1990s, Peru had lost its status as the world's leading coca producer, as the Colombian drugs mafias began to grow their own leaves. Colombia, not previously a large producer of coca, quickly overtook Peru in terms of output. Coca acreage in Peru peaked in 1992 at around 240,000 hectares, and began to fall thereafter. The decline in Peruvian production was aided by the collapse of *Sendero*, which made it easier for the government in Lima to pursue the eradication and

▼ *A street market in Ayacucho. The sacks contain coca leaves, sold for personal consumption amongst the local population.*

Susana Pastor

crop substitution programmes demanded by Washington. Output also fell because of the appearance of a fungus that attacked the roots of coca plants, and which spread rapidly through the Alto Huallaga region. Mainly because of the increase in Colombian production, the price of coca fell sharply. As coca became less profitable, peasant farmers became more willing to contemplate farming alternative crops, particularly when this attracted outside assistance and made for a more tranquil existence.

One of the main alternatives to coca was coffee. In the mid-1990s, as coca prices fell, the world price of coffee was in the ascendant. Backed by USAID and others, peasants were given technical assistance to improve the quality and quantity of coffee plantations. These expanded as the area planted with coca shrank, a development applauded in Washington as a sign that the USA was winning the 'war on drugs'. The US government, which had criticised Fujimori's palace coup in 1992, began to warm to *fujimorismo*. Success in decreasing coca production also improved relations between Montesinos and branches of the US government like the Drug Enforcement Administration (DEA), and his old friends at the CIA. Though his methods were somewhat suspect, they seemed to be having some effect. It only became clear later that Montesinos was playing a double game. At the same time as he pursued the eradication programme, he was receiving pay-offs from business-people with an interest in keeping the Peruvian coca industry alive. Many of his colleagues in the armed forces were also on the make.

Success in crop substitution was short-lived. Market prices for coffee beans slumped in the late 1990s, mainly because of a glut in the world market caused by huge increases in supply from Brazil and Vietnam. Coca prices, meanwhile, began to recover. The average price for a kilo of coca leaves in the 1995-98 period was US$0.40. By 2000, it had risen to US$2.80, and at the end of 2001 the price stood at US$3-3.50 a kilo. By 2001, a hectare of coca would generate roughly ten times the income of a hectare of coffee. In large part, the rise in coca prices was due to the US-backed 'Plan Colombia', one of the effects of which was to encourage Colombian coca purchasers to buy from Peru. The rise in prices led to a sharp increase in coca planting in Peru.

According to US figures, the area planted with coca in Peru increased from 34,100 hectares in 2000 to 52,000 hectares in 2001. Peruvian drug authorities put the 2001 figure at 65,000 hectares, of which 30-35,000 hectares were in the Huallaga region, 18-20,000 in the Apurímac valley further south, and 12,000 in La Convención/

IN SEARCH OF GREEN GOLD

The Alto Mayo is one of Peru's best coffee producing areas. The soil is rich, and at around 1350 metres, the altitude is optimal for high-grade coffees. The village of Roque, perched high above the Mayo river, enjoys commanding views over this wide, lush, green valley. The *Oro Verde* ('Green Gold') co-operative is trying to organise workers there to improve the quality of their coffee. But it is a losing battle, because coca is the new 'green gold'. Villagers are selling up and moving down to the Huallaga valley to work on the coca plantations. Even those who stay are finding it increasingly difficult to harvest the coffee crop: labour is scarce, and no-one is willing to harvest coffee. In Roque, and other places like it, households fragment as men migrate to earn money picking coca lower down in the valley, leaving women and children at home to manage the family farm as best they can.

Lares in Cuzco. The US estimates, based mainly on aerial photography, do not take differences in yields fully into account. On the basis of estimated yields, the main production area appears to have shifted to the Apurímac valley (which is unaffected by the coca fungus). Growers there harvest around 2000 kg per hectare, as opposed to 800 kg in Alto Huallaga, and 500 kg in La Convención. According to those working in the Apurímac valley, growers are receiving all the technical advice and financial and other inputs they need from the Colombian *narcos*. At the same time, the cultivation of opium poppies, used for manufacturing heroin, was on the increase in the highland areas of Cajamarca and Piura. Here, too, the clamp-down in Colombia created knock-on effects in Peru.

CASHING IN

Susana Pastor

Trucks laden with fruit zig-zag up the serpentine road linking San Francisco, in the Apurímac valley, and the city of Ayacucho. *En route*, they pass through a series of police checkpoints. For local policemen, the checkpoints are the best assignment around, and competition to man them is strong. Following payment of a suitable fee, the lorries' clandestine coca cargoes are waved through, and the police return home feeling well-rewarded.

World Vision, an international evangelical NGO, has worked for many years in the valley of the Apurímac, assisting the return of people to communities abandoned during the violence of the 1980s. In the 1980s, coca production was the only real source of growth in the Ayacuchan economy. In the 1990s, crop substitution money was showered on places like Palmapampa. But by the end of the decade, with coca prices recovering fast, Palmapampa had reverted to its former status as the region's coca capital. *Sendero*, which has maintained a constant presence in the area, is once again active in the communities of the valley. It poses as a defender of the local *cocaleros* against new inroads by the coca eradicators. According to Víctor Belleza at World Vision, coca eradication is not impossible, but it would require a development strategy that brings industry to the area. 'It would need to go well beyond agriculture', he says, and adds that, 'Ultimately this depends on political will.'

Affirming rights

Susana Pastor

▲ *During the worst years of violence, many rural people had to seek refuge in the towns and cities, disrupting their traditional ways of life. All through the troubled years, the Pérez family never ceased to hold their annual fiesta, even in exile. As a result, their fiesta is intimately related with the struggle, and with the family's gradual homecoming to their ancestral lands in Sanya, Ayacucho.*

The human cost of war

No-one knows for sure how many people were killed or 'disappeared' during the twelve-year war between Sendero Luminoso and the Peruvian armed forces. What is clear is that the great majority were innocent bystanders caught in the cross-fire of this merciless conflict. After the collapse of the Fujimori regime, one of the first actions of the interim Paniagua government was to order a Truth and Reconciliation Commission to investigate human rights violations during the conflict period. The Commission began its unsavoury task of piecing together the story shortly after Alejandro Toledo became president in July 2001.

The Commission's brief states that it should investigate all cases of human rights violation between 1980-2000; from the time that Sendero lobbed its first bomb at Chuschi until the end of the Fujimori period. It therefore covers three presidencies: not just that of Alberto Fujimori (1990-2000), but also those of Fernando Belaunde (1980-85) and Alan García (1985-90). A chronology published for this period by DESCO, a research NGO in Lima, claims that there were 24,000 deaths and 4200 'disappearances'. Forty per cent of these killings took place in Ayacucho. This tally is based only on known cases; the real figure is probably much higher. According to José Coronel, an anthropologist who leads the Commission in Ayacucho, new cases of killings were every day coming to light as the Commission started to interview people in the villages affected by violence. 'Almost every community has its own list of those killed or disappeared', he says.

In Ayacucho, as well as in neighbouring Apurímac and Huancavelica, Sendero was responsible for most of the deaths that occurred at higher altitudes. For several years, Sendero was able to establish a 'liberated zone' in the highest, poorest, and most remote communities; local state authorities within the zone were killed or banished. The armed forces made forays into such areas, but they were intermittent. Where they held sway, *Senderistas* dealt summarily with those who they believed stood in their way. Either people were with them or against them; there was no middle way. The death toll was highest in those parts of the *sierra* where Sendero encountered resistance. This was the case, for instance, in the Razhuilca *massif* to the north of Ayacucho city. The scars borne by the villagers of Huayllay are typical of those of the region as a whole. Sendero terrorised the highland communities to rally support in its war against the Peruvian state. The village of Uchuraccay, close to Huayllay, became famous when eight journalists were killed there in 1983, investigating a story that the locals were turning against Sendero. It was typical of this war, waged far from the capital or other urban centres, that the killings of thousands of peasants attracted little public attention. Human rights violations aroused more controversy and received more media exposure when the victims were city dwellers, not *campesinos*.

The counter-insurgency response to Sendero was to meet violence with violence, terror with terror. Initially, this was the task given to a paramilitary police brigade, known as the 'sinchis' (*sinchi* means 'all-powerful' in Quechua). The *sinchis* played into Sendero's hands by running amok, and offending local opinion in Ayacucho and other towns through their arbitrary and abusive behaviour. When the *sinchis* failed to curb the insurgency, Belaunde brought in the military in 1982. Political authority was vested in a local military commander with wide-ranging powers to do what he thought best to finish Sendero. The army, and to a lesser extent the marines, took this mandate literally, developing a regime of counter-terror to win back peasant loyalties. Lacking the means to collect systematic intelligence about their adversaries, troops would frequently respond with indiscriminate violence. Soldiers, recruited mainly from the coast, were encouraged to think of Quechua-speaking *campesinos* as inferior beings. In turn, the troops became targets for attack by a guerrilla enemy they could not identify. On occasions, in retribution, the army resorted to massacring whole communities. 'Disappearances' became common, and torture, rape, and arson were standard practice. In the town of Huanta, two hours

▼ *Michel and Samuel Pacheco, from Huayllay, show us how to use the* chaquitaclla, *the traditional digging tool. Michel and Samuel are lucky — their parents are still alive; many children were orphaned during the violence.*

Susana Pastor

north of Ayacucho, the troops became particularly notorious for their abuse of basic human rights. It was to Huanta that villagers from Huayllay were taken, never to return.

Massacre at Cayara

On 14 May 1988, troops arrived at the small town of Cayara, to the south of Ayacucho, by helicopter and road. A few days before, Senderistas had killed four soldiers nearby. The troops tortured and then executed 29 members of the community in revenge, including the local schoolteacher, and a number of schoolchildren. Five people were taken into the church and hacked to death with clubs and machetes.

This is the account of an 11-year old boy who witnessed what happened and lived to tell the tale, as recounted in the words of the public prosecutor. 'Soldiers wearing black ski masks, armed with heavy weapons... made his father lie on the ground. One kicked him while another hit him with the butt of a gun. He clung to his father and told the soldiers that his father was innocent, but the soldiers threatened him with a cattle whip.... He didn't want to look back after he heard someone cry.... They were trampling on his father. The boy cried out in Quechua that they were killing him.... He didn't see his father again. Later the soldiers told him to get away, and he ran with the women. One later told him that they had cut off his father's head.'

Because of this and other testimonies, the Cayara killings caused a major national uproar. The Senate sent a commission to investigate what had happened. The García government and the military authorities did their utmost to obstruct the investigation. Witnesses were killed and intimidated, and evidence removed. In its report on what happened, the Senate commission ended by saying that no criminal acts had been committed that day in Cayara.

False justice

With the arrest in 1992 of Abimael Guzmán, Sendero's supreme leader and ideologue, the nature of the human rights violations began to change. Sendero's military capacity crumbled as, one after another, its leaders were identified and arrested. By offering lighter sentences to those who identified their comrades in arms, the authorities were able to round up large numbers of suspects. But to save their own skins, many of those accused simply named anyone they could think of. The numbers of those unjustly held began to rise. Changes to the legal code governing cases of terrorism, passed in the wake of Fujimori's 1992 palace coup, made 'terrorism' and 'treason' offences punishable by death.

The Fujimori administration turned to military tribunals to judge those accused of terrorism. In these, the evidence of witnesses and other norms of proof were cast aside in the desire for rapid 'justice'.

Susana Pastor

▲ *Víctor Quispe explains how the complex web of symbols in Edwin Sulca's tapestry represents a personal interpretation of Peru's recent history. 'Those of us from Ayacucho who did not want war, they tied our hands.... Amongst the bombs... we heard the cries of orphans, of mothers, of women burying their dead. All this brought us to our knees.... Now the campesinos have hope. They will return to the fields, and the maize will flourish once more.'*

The accused, usually lacking any proper defence, were unable to see those who passed judgement on them, seated behind one-way mirrors. It was only towards the end of the Fujimori regime that, under strong international pressure, a commission was appointed to review the cases of thousands of innocent people wrongly committed, and mostly serving life sentences.

The issue of wrongful arrest focused public attention on conditions in Peru's prisons. Peruvian jails have long had a bad reputation. They are overcrowded, and lack even the most basic guarantees for prisoner safety. Prisoners depend on outside support from friends and family to acquire even minimal needs like food. Some prisons are deliberately located in inhospitable places – at very high altitudes, or in the jungle. The International Red Cross has criticised Peru for failing to hold prisoners in reasonable conditions and for suspending their visiting rights. Protests by inmates, especially by Sendero prisoners, have been dealt with summarily. In 1986, for instance, García responded to a synchronised rebellion in three Lima prisons by sending in troops. Some 400 prisoners were killed.

The appointment of the Truth and Reconciliation Commission, which is due to report its findings in 2003, provides an important opportunity to overcome this grim legacy. As well as detailing the facts of what happened, the Commission will seek to explain why they happened, and what can be done in the future to restore a sense of justice. However, it will not pass judgement on those it identifies as responsible; nor will it make reparations for the injustices committed. The identities of those who committed human rights atrocities will be, in any case, difficult to establish. Both the military and Sendero took steps to disguise those involved in attacks. Members of the armed forces, offered amnesty by Fujimori in 1995, are likely to claim that they were simply following orders and had no alternative but to do as they did. Also, as Coronel points out, 'The reconstruction of memory as to exactly what happened is fraught with difficulty.' Although justice may never be done, the Commission's work is nevertheless important. 'It's a kind of catharsis for the families of the victims,' Coronel says, helping them to come to terms with their grief.

▲ *Soldiers move to police a demonstration in Ayacucho.*

Criminality, the police, and the justice system

The era of extreme fear and insecurity associated with Sendero Luminoso may be over, but most Peruvians continue to feel insecure and ill-protected by the state. Common crime – assault, robbery, kidnapping, and even murder – is all-pervasive, and the problem appears to be getting worse. Sociologists attribute this to the combined effects of poverty and urbanisation. Reacting to this climate of violence, the residents of wealthy neighbourhoods have started to surround their homes with high walls, installing video surveillance cameras and employing armed guards to provide protection. Factories in many parts of Lima now look like mini-fortresses, with walls, observation turrets, and searchlights. Ordinary people, however, are unable to go to such lengths to protect themselves, and it is they who bear the brunt of the rising tide of violent crime.

In poor neighbourhoods of Lima, like San Juan de Lurigancho and Pamplona Alta, residents live in trepidation at the activities of local gangs which, after nightfall, take over the streets. The gangs are typically formed of groups of adolescent boys with little prospect of a better future. Each neighbourhood in San Juan de Lurigancho has a gang, and each gang disputes with other gangs over the control of territory. Drug consumption and trafficking is linked with increased gang violence. Gang members are forced to show that they can kill, while those reluctant to get involved are often beaten up and threatened. Long knives and handguns, easily obtained, are the arms of choice. In some areas, like Matupe in San Juan de Lurigancho, terrified residents club together to contract guards with dogs to defend the streets. 'These gangs are mafias in the making,' says a social worker in Pamplona Alta, where NGOs are trying to teach residents methods of violence prevention.

People would normally turn to the police for protection in such circumstances. However, in large parts of San Juan – especially in the peripheral areas where communities are poorest and least organised – the police are nowhere to be seen after nightfall. For many, indeed, the police are part of the problem rather than the solution. The police force is poorly paid, and confronts a social problem which it cannot begin to solve. In Lima and elsewhere, police morale is low, and bribery and corruption in the force are commonplace. Many believe that the police are themselves involved in acts of organised crime.

In rural areas, too, communities receive little external help in defending their rights. Police stations tend to be located in towns and cities, not villages. Where there is a police presence, it tends to be seen as part of a power structure that is irredeemably corrupt. When Sendero Luminoso

▲ *Municipal security forces are a frequent sight on the streets of central Lima.*

removed a local policeman after attacking a community, this would sometimes be regarded as a positive development by the villagers; in rural areas, the police have come to symbolise all that is most abusive and corrupt about the state. Police reform has been identified by the Toledo government as one of its most urgent priorities, and there is much that needs to be done.

The justice system, too, seldom works to the advantage of those most in need of it. Like policemen, lawyers and judges have a poor reputation in Peru, mainly because they are seen as working in the interests of those who can pay the biggest bribes. The court system is itself labyrinthine, inefficient, and costly to those looking for justice. As an old adage about Lima's impressive-looking Palace of Justice goes, there's a lot of palace, but precious little justice. Because judges are political appointments, the justice system has tended not to protect the interests of individuals, particularly those with scant resources, against the state. Rather, it has protected those in government who have acted corruptly, defending private interests over the public good. In any case, for most Peruvians, the justice system is simply too expensive to access; other methods are therefore found to settle legal disputes. In rural areas, the justice system seldom extends beyond the confines of provincial or district capitals, providing no solutions to rural people when they need mediation in pressing matters like land or family disputes.

Peru has consistently been criticised in international forums over the shortcomings of its justice system. Amnesty International has been among its most persistent critics over the abuse of human rights, and the impunity afforded to those responsible. The Inter-American Court of Human Rights, based in San José in Costa Rica, has also been highly critical of Peru on human rights grounds. It was because of its persistence on a range of issues that the Fujimori government took the unusual step of publicly withdrawing Peru from the jurisdiction of the Court. Yet, the importance of judicial reform has long been recognised. The need to end corruption in the justice system was one of Fujimori's justifications for his 1992 palace coup. Apart from questions of finance, the problem seems to lie in the convenience to governments (of whatever political colour) of having a judiciary that can be counted on to do its bidding. But as people become more aware of their rights and assertive in defending them, things are gradually beginning to change.

COMMUNITY JUSTICE

In rural communities, a novel system is being introduced by the Justice Ministry (with the help of NGOs) to enable community leaders to dispense justice. These are the *Nucleos Rurales de Administración de Justicia* ('Rural Nuclei for the Administration of Justice'). The NURAJ, as they are known, are an unusual example of judicial reform from the bottom up. They started as a pilot scheme in the Ayacuchan provinces of Huanta and Vilcashuamán, because of the absence of judicial authorities there. They deal with the need for judgements on frequent problems, such as land disputes, animal theft, family violence, and sexual harassment. According to Jeffrey Gamarra, who has been one of the main initiators of the scheme, it has been a great success in providing justice for those who could never afford to seek it from a judge in Ayacucho.

A right to education

New orange-painted school buildings, bearing plaques of gratitude to 'Eng. Alberto Fujimori, Constitutional President of the Republic', are a familiar sight in communities, rural and urban. Orange was the adopted colour of Fujimori's *Cambio-90* political grouping, and school-building formed a key part of his attempts to win public favour. But the programme of school building by itself was not enough to cure Peru's ailing education system. Poor families had no money to buy schoolbooks, and the government was unwilling to give the education ministry the budget to pay teachers a living wage. The result was that in many places, especially in rural areas, brand new schools were used, not for teaching children, but as storage areas or even cowsheds.

Ever since the 1950s, when the first massive school expansion programme took place in Peru, education has been seen as one of the keys to social mobility. Organisations like the World Bank have repeatedly argued that improving education is the most important policy tool in assisting people to escape from poverty. It is possible, at least theoretically,

► *Government workers on the roof of the new school building in Santo Domingo, Piura*

Annie Bungeroth

for children from poor backgrounds to acquire the knowledge to get beyond primary school and to receive secondary or even university education. The possibility of attaining a university education became a dream harboured by many, and some have managed to use education to open doors that would otherwise have remained shut. Alejandro Toledo is a case in point. From humble rural origins in Ancash, he managed to work his way up the educational system, eventually completing a doctorate at Stanford University in the USA.

But the reality is rather different for all but a small minority. Less than 60 per cent of those in state schools finish grade eleven, and the numbers that reach university are tiny. Though state schools do not charge fees, the quality of the education they provide is poor, and those who can afford it send their children to private schools or to schools run by the Catholic Church. The public education system emphasises old-fashioned approaches like rote learning, rather than developing other skills. For the majority, the educational system fails to equip them to get better jobs when they leave school. School drop-out rates are high, especially among girls. When families have to economise they are more likely to send boys than girls to school, and girls are often called to assist with the care of siblings and other household tasks. In San Juan de Lurigancho, the drop-out rate is around 15 per cent on average, but more in the poorest neighbourhoods. Rates are also higher in rural areas, where the quality of education is worst, and children are often required to work on the land rather than attend school. Far from being a right, education is often seen by parents as an expensive burden that they are obliged to assume. Even 'free' education entails buying schoolbooks, materials, and uniforms. For those living on $1-2 a day, it is impossible to meet such expenses.

Overall, illiteracy is fairly low for a developing country, but it is high in rural areas, and particularly among women. More than a quarter of women living in rural areas of the *sierra* were officially classified as illiterate in 2000, and more than 20 per cent in rural parts of the jungle. Overall, women are three times more likely to be illiterate than men, which means that they are less likely ever to escape poverty.

The education ministry's budget accounted for seven per cent of total government spending in 2000, small by contrast with the 39 per cent spent on servicing Peru's foreign debt. The school-building programme came under the ministry of the presidency, however. Educational spending peaked in the mid-80s at the beginning of the García government, but tailed off in subsequent years. A large proportion of the education budget is spent on teachers' wages, and these have fallen sharply. The teachers' union, SUTEP, has been unable to maintain the real value of teachers' pay. True to its Maoist convictions, SUTEP was highly critical of Fujimori and his government. As trained teachers seek other occupations outside education, the numbers in the profession are ever lower in comparison with the numbers of children entering the public education system.

A right to health

Peru – like most countries in Latin America – has seen some improvement in basic health indicators in recent decades. Life expectancy, for instance, has increased steadily since the 1960s. In spite of higher levels of poverty and inequality, the average Peruvian man can expect to live to 67 (compared with 57, 20 years ago), whilst the average woman will live to 72 (compared with 61, 20 years ago). The number of children who die in infancy has also fallen fairly dramatically, from 99 per 1000 live births 20 years ago to around 45 today. The number of hospitals, clinics, and medical posts has increased.

In other respects, recent trends make for less encouraging reading. Cholera, absent from Peru since the early years of the 20th century, made a dramatic comeback in the early 1990s, revealing yawning inadequacies in the system of public health control. Diseases most closely associated with poverty – notably tuberculosis – have remained prevalent, while the incidence of respiratory diseases, and dysentery increased sharply in the late 1990s. Other diseases thought to be on the wane – such as malaria and dengue – have also staged a comeback. Furthermore, the health system has found itself having to cope with new diseases, like HIV and AIDS, as well as the chronic ailments associated with an ageing population. The official figures for AIDS (11,700 cases between 1983 and 2001), as well as those for other diseases, almost certainly under-report their true incidence.

Health-care provision has suffered as a product of the debt crisis and the IMF-imposed fiscal austerity in recent years. Health spending has long been low in Peru by Latin American standards, both as a proportion of government spending and as a percentage of GDP. Social spending as a whole (mainly health and education) fell from 4.7 per cent of GDP in 1980 to 2.1 per cent in 1995. With debt repayment and military spending absorbing a large part of overall public expenditure, health has only accounted for between four and five per cent of budget outlays in recent years, a lower proportion than in most other Latin American countries. In the 2002 budget, debt servicing was estimated to cost considerably more than twice health and education together.

Susana Pastor

▲ *Ayacuchan members of the education union, SUTEP, march in support of a national strike. According to the local SUTEP leader, 'We're protesting against the regional education authority, which has not been listening to the demands from qualified teachers for fair salaries and pensions, or from contractors who have not been paid for the last four months.' SUTEP is one of Peru's most militant unions.*

The overall figures also mask profound inequalities in health-care provision, both socially and regionally. The average rate for infant mortality in the 1995-2000 period was 45 per 1000 live births, while in Ayacucho it was 67, and in Huancavelica 86. In 2000, 40 per cent of children under the age of five in rural parts of the *sierra* showed stunted growth because of malnutrition, but only 7.7 per cent in greater Lima. There were 23.9 hospital beds for every 10,000 citizens in Lima in 1996, compared with only 8.3 in Cajamarca and in Puno. Similarly, there were 18.9 doctors for 10,000 people in Lima, but only 2.8 in Huancavelica and 2.9 in Apurímac. The system of health care in Peru is highly skewed towards urban hospital provision at the expense of rural areas, even though, under Fujimori, a greater proportion of health spending went on rural health posts. As with schools, many of these new health posts lack the basic materials to tackle simple health problems.

▼ *A young woman washes her hands under a newly-installed standpipe in Piura. Clean water is essential for public health.*

Annie Bungeroth

The quality of health provision also varies dramatically between different sectors of the population. The health ministry provides for those sectors with least resources, covering the medical needs of around two-thirds of the population. Health ministry hospitals are the worst-equipped, and the treatment they provide is the most basic. This sector is particularly exposed to cuts in public spending. The Peruvian Social Security Institute caters for those in employment who contribute to health insurance through their wages. This sector has also suffered from cuts in state provision. Declining standards of attention are increasingly pushing those who can afford to do so to buy private health insurance to gain access to private hospitals and clinics. The quality of medical attention in these is far superior to public sector hospitals, but they cater only for a few well-off patients.

Access to health care is therefore a function of income rather than a right that stems from citizenship. Those who are poor are either excluded altogether – only five out of every ten women giving birth receive any medical attention – or receive very inferior attention to those who can afford to pay. According to Mario Ríos at the human rights organisation APRODEH, health provision will only improve when people start to demand better health care as a right. 'Those who least claim their rights are precisely those who need them most,' he says. 'There is very little even by way of public

▲ *Lazunda Dominguez Castillo tends the camomile plants in her garden.*

HERBAL REMEDIES

Owing to the expense of buying pharmaceutical medicines, more and more people on low incomes are resorting to herbal remedies as an alternative. Even the health ministry is now beginning to take more notice of remedies that only a few years ago would have been laughed at as the delusions of witch-doctors and quacks. Peru has a rich stock of experience in the use of such remedies, but these traditions are at risk of being lost if the older generation of Peruvians, with their roots in the countryside, does not pass them on to the younger. NGOs, like CEDAP in Ayacucho, are working on ways to maximise the benefits of traditional forms of treatment. They report a large increase in the use of medicinal herbs, to the benefit of peasant growers. At Coyona in Piura, Margarita Chuquipoma, the vice-president of the local Mothers' Club, dedicates herself full-time to her herb garden. She says she will only consult a doctor if an illness is really serious. Most problems, she says, are best treated with time-honoured cures.

information on how to access the health system.' In response to such problems, local health committees came into being in the mid-1990s to channel pressure from below. Their success, however, has depended on the level of people's determination, and the strength of their community organisation. The most successful are not usually those from the poorest neighbourhoods. The Toledo government has promised to reform the health system, but a lack of funding remains the main obstacle to better provision.

Women's rights

The women of San Juan de Lurigancho are learning leadership skills. Three days a week for two terms a year, 50 women abandon their other activities to learn how to be future councillors, mayors, or even congress-women. 'This is the only way forward to creating real citizenship in our community,' says Luzmilla de la Cruz, vice-chair of the local association of *comedores*. With a little outside help, the *comedores* have gone from providing food to the neighbourhood to involving the community in matters such as food distribution, health provision, and providing for local security needs. Future leadership courses will include themes as diverse as globalisation, active citizenship, and budgetary planning.

WELL-BEING FOR WOMEN

The *Casa del Bien-estar* ('Home of Well-being') in Pamplona Alta, in southern Lima, opened its doors to the public in 1997. Until then, there was no assistance available to women in this neighbourhood of 80,000 people. The pharmacy at the *Casa* offers basic medicines, mostly for treatment of reproductive health problems. Although not free, drugs are priced to be affordable. A course of pills to treat a vaginal infection costs 2 *soles* (around 40 pence), for example.

The centre also has a clinic, a laboratory to examine specimens, a credit facility, and a legal advice bureau. 'We seek to identify the difficulties people have in getting help from the state,' says Rocío Gutiérrez, 'and to give them the confidence to stand up for themselves.' The centre plays a key role in the life of Pamplona Alta, helping thousands of women each year.

Gender-based organisations, aimed at increasing respect for women's rights, have multiplied in Peru since the 1980s. They have been helped along by the activities of organisations such as *Flora Tristán, Manuela Ramos*, and *Incafam*. All of these NGOs support programmes in rural and urban areas. One of their core areas of activity has been reproductive health. Although women today are more able than their predecessors to confront such problems in an open way, a great deal still needs to be done. 'Sexuality, maternity, and questions like reproductive health have to be placed as new issues in the public sphere', says Flora Tristán's María Emma Manarelli. 'We need to create whole new areas of public discussion.' Through its publications and its publicity machine, Flora Tristán has helped to shape this new agenda. The problem, Manarelli argues, lies in the hierarchical and male-oriented (*machista*) cultural tradition in Peru, which is extremely resistant to change. She also cites Catholic resistance to adequate birth control programmes.

Some women's organisations are positive about the contribution of the Fujimori regime, at least in two respects. Fujimori established a separate ministry for women's affairs, putting it in charge of the PRONAA food distribution programme. Although PRONAA undoubtedly lent itself to political manipulation, the ministry also gave women's issues greater salience at the cabinet level. Secondly, Fujimori pursued a proactive policy on birth control, making contraceptives much more readily available. In low-income urban neighbourhoods, in particular, sexual activity begins at an early age, and the incidence of unwanted pregnancies is very high.

Susana Pastor

▼ *Carmen Campos, from Chulucanas, explains how women's involvement in local development organisations like the* comedores *can put them at risk of increased violence from their husbands.*

Annie Bungeroth

A Lima hospital reports 5000 pregnancies each year among girls between the ages of 12 and 17, and most are a consequence of rape, often by male relatives. There is little guidance available for young women on how to avoid pregnancy, and the incidence of abortion is high. According to Flora Tristán, as many as 35 per cent of all pregnancies end in abortion, and the lack of adequate facilities puts women at risk of death from botched back-street abortions.

Susana Pastor

▲ *The mural, painted by college students from Pamplona Alta, calls for an end to sexual violence. It says: 'Remaining silent is no solution'.*

The ugly side of Fujimori's population policy was its pursuit of forced sterilisation programmes in order to lower the birth rate. No-one knows for sure how many women were obliged to undergo surgical sterilisation, but the practice was common in rural areas, where the birth rate is far higher than in towns and cities. Social workers were given cash bonuses for the number of women they could cajole into taking part into such programmes, and the operations were frequently conducted by inexperienced doctors in unhygienic conditions. The Catholic Church was energetic in criticising such programmes, but to little immediate avail. However, the outcry over sterilisation eventually forced the state to abandon this as official policy.

Family and sexual violence are other major perennial problems that feminist organisations seek to address. In 1999, there were 9000 reported cases of domestic violence, but this is probably just a small fraction of the real total. There are few places where women (poor women in particular) can go to seek help or refuge from violence. One of the aims of the leadership school in San Juan de Lurigancho is to explain to ordinary women what they should do when their rights are violated in these ways. One avenue is to secure legal advice, but legal action is usually slow and ineffectual. Another is to seek refuge, but there are only five refuge centres in Lima, for a population of eight million. The most common response is to seek a sympathetic ear and a some practical advice. This is what is offered to people attending the family help centre in Pamplona Alta, a project set up by Manuela Ramos.

Indigenous rights

Unlike Bolivia and Ecuador, Peru lacks a strong pro-indigenous (*indigenista*) tradition, even though a large proportion of the population is of indigenous descent. The political tradition of highland Indians is more versed in concepts of class struggle (*clasismo*) than ethnic identity. For peasant confederations, like the Peruvian Peasant Confederation (CCP), the main ideological reference point has been the work of José Carlos Mariátegui, the founder of the Peruvian Communist Party, whose writings stressed the need for Marxist orthodoxy to take on board the revolutionary potential of peasants. Although the figure of Túpac Amaru, the leader of the largest indigenous revolt against the Spanish empire in the 1780s (his real name was José Gabriel Condorcanqui), was part of the iconography of the Velasco regime, it was used more as a symbol of national independence than a statement of indigenous values. The guerrilla *Movimiento Revolucionario Túpac Amaru* (MRTA) did likewise, but its main ideological inspiration was the Cuban revolution. For its part, Sendero Luminoso based its revolutionary praxis on an extreme interpretation of *clasismo*.

It is to the lowland indigenous groups of the Amazon forests that we must look for the main expression of *indigenismo* in Peru. There are some 60 different indigenous peoples living in the jungles of Peru, belonging to 14 main linguistic families. They represent only a small proportion of the total population of Peru, less than 240,000 people according to the 1993 census. The largest grouping is the Aguaruna nation, concentrated in the northern departments of Amazonas, Cajamarca, San Martín, and Loreto.

▼ *A gathering of the leaders of Bajo Naranjillo, members of the Aguaruna people. The mayor told us, 'There should be a ministry for indigenous peoples in Peru. The ministry would defend Amazonia on our behalf. With this support, maybe the indigenous communities will survive, and gain national and international recognition.'*

Susana Pastor

▲ *Women wash clothes in Bajo Naranjillo. The river flows on to join the waters of the Amazon.*

The next largest group is the Campa-Asháninka, who live primarily in Junín, Pasco, Cuzco, and Ucayali. The indigenous peoples of Amazonia are represented at the national level by, amongst others, AIDESEP (*Asociación Inter-étnica de la Selva Peruana*). AIDESEP has six regional offices in the jungle, but also provides a national lobbying forum. It claims to represent 1340 different communities in the jungle.

Prime among AIDESEP's demands is the recognition of autonomy for indigenous communities. It wants the constitutional article that defines Peru as 'pluricultural and multiethnic' to be given real meaning. According to Wrays Pérez from AIDESEP, this could signify, for example, ensuring some permanent indigenous representation in Congress. One of the problems facing jungle Indians is that they are so few in number, and so spread out over different departments, that it is impossible for them to register their own political party. The lack of any demarcation between indigenous lands also makes representation more difficult.

AIDESEP and other pro-indigenous organisations thus strive to protect both indigenous landholding, and their cultural value systems. Lowland tribes find their lands continually penetrated by outsiders, whether migrants from the *sierra*, gold explorers, timber companies, or companies exploring for oil and gas. It is not just a problem of land, but also the defence of the subsoil, and the wealth contained within it. Where oil is extracted, for instance, Indians would like to establish rights that would ensure they receive some of the benefits. Communities also demand the protection of their culture through bilingual education, and approaches to health care sensitive to long-held traditional values.

Jungle Indians have never had much impact on national politics in Peru. However, the interest shown by international companies in developing the resources of Amazonia is giving them increased political leverage. They have come to exert considerable influence over the development of gas and oil reserves, for example. In 1996, protests by the Ashuar people led to ARCO being stopped from developing an oilfield in the jungle. The Camisea gas project has also forced multinational companies to respond to indigenous concerns. Pérez believes that Toledo is better-disposed towards indigenous rights than Fujimori ever was, mainly because his Belgian-born wife, a Quechua-speaking anthropologist, is keen to promote them.

The natural environment

As you approach the town of Tambo Grande in the department of Piura, roadside signs tell you that life is worth more than gold. Far from an abstract statement of philosophical or religious belief, the words are full of current political meaning. Living on top of a large gold deposit, the people of Tambo Grande are determined to stop a mining project that would destroy a substantial part of their town. Far from being a boon to people in this part of Piura, the Tambo Grande project is viewed as a direct threat to their livelihoods and way of life. Tambo Grande is the main town in the San Lorenzo valley, and the area has a population of around 70,000. Although the history of Tambo Grande stretches back to Inca times, the valley first became agriculturally important in the 1950s, as a result of a World Bank irrigation project. For 40 years, small-scale producers in San Lorenzo have shown the way in exporting agricultural goods, notably mangoes, lemons, limes, tamarind, avocados, and oranges. The people of the area fear that, if developed, the gold mine will not only spell the end of Tambo Grande as a town, but will ruin the agriculture of the region through air and water pollution. Determined to stop the project going ahead, they say they will put their lives on the line if need be.

Other than the mining company involved – a Canadian firm called Manhattan – the locals' main adversary seems to be the government in Lima. The Toledo administration is under pressure, from the IMF and others, to leave no stone unturned in the quest to attract foreign investment and maximise export earnings. If Peru is to repay its debts and increase its international reserves, then – the argument goes – it needs to attract foreign investment and increase its exports. Tambo Grande is one of a number of mining projects where foreign companies are evaluating the economic possibilities. Geologists believe that Tambo Grande may be part of a much larger area of gold deposits in the eastern part of Piura. Such prospects, of course, have aroused the attention of business interests in the capital of the Piura region, where some see the project as a way to make money.

▼ The slogans on this Tambo Grande building read 'Mango: work for all', and 'Development with agriculture, without mining'.

Susana Pastor

THE BATTLE FOR TAMBO GRANDE

The Manhattan company publicity video describes Tambo Grande as a town 'looking towards the future', and portrays agriculture and mining as an 'an alliance for sustainable development'. The mine, it says, will go forward on the basis of 'citizen participation'. Not so, says Francisco Ojeda, the president of the Tambo Grande Defence Front. In his view, the mine would be an ecological disaster of huge proportions, ending San Lorenzo's hard-won battle to win foreign export markets for its prized mangoes and lemons. As for consultation and participation, he says, Manhattan has pursued its project behind the backs of the local people.

The planned open-cast pit would be 1 km long, 750 metres wide, and 300 metres deep. It would cover an area of 75 hectares, and involve the demolition of 1600 homes, and displacement of 8000 people. The building of a refinery would take up another 15 hectares. The project would divert the course of the Piura River, which runs through the town.

The company film says that there would be no contamination, and that the mine would not take a 'drop of water' from the San Lorenzo reservoir that serves the valley's agricultural needs. 'This is nonsense', says Ojeda, 'dust from the project will contaminate all our crops', pointing also to the toxicity of the chemicals used in refining gold. Whatever the technology ultimately used, NGOs in Piura doubt the government's ability to ensure compliance with environmental standards.

The Defence Front has rallied local opinion in the San Lorenzo valley, and lobbied hard both in the regional capital and in Lima. In June 2002, it prevailed in holding a local referendum on the issue, in which Manhattan's proposals were decisively rejected.

▼ *The poster reads, 'Imagine cebiche without lemon'. Cebiche is a famous typical Peruvian dish, made of fish marinated in lemon juice. Tambo Grande residents fear the mine will destroy the flourishing local lemon industry.*

Tambo Grande is emblematic of the conflicts of interests that investment projects can generate. Their resolution is not just a question of environmental impact assessments, but, ultimately, of political decisions. Few other mining projects in the *sierra* are situated as close to human habitation or areas of agricultural wealth as Tambo Grande. Traditionally, most mines have been located in the high Andes, where agriculture is of low productivity. These projects have affected poor peasants who lack the political clout of the Tambo Grande Defence Front. Striking the right balance between the need to export and the need to protect the interests of local people is often difficult. Powerful interests are involved, and in the past, mining companies in Peru have been notoriously insensitive towards the interests of those who they consider to be 'getting in the way of progress'. Such conflicts can be dangerous for those involved: in Tambo Grande, one of the Front's main leaders was killed in mysterious circumstances in 2001. Manhattan denies that it was in any way involved in this killing. Although his death may have been wholly unrelated to his activism, many local people fear that it was not just an accident.

Peru's perennial need for foreign exchange means that economic opportunities in any sector are seized upon with little thought for the longer-term consequences. The fishing boom of the early 1970s, for instance, ended in lengthy bans on fishing: exploitation of Peru's marine resources led to the exhaustion of stocks. Towns like Chimbote profited from the fish bonanza, attracting huge flows of migrants, only to become areas of mass unemployment when the fishing industry collapsed. The application of 'green revolution' technologies in agriculture – such as high-yielding varieties of seed, and increased use of irrigation and agro-chemicals – had rather similar effects. Initially, agricultural yields rose substantially, but then the improved yields decreased as the quality of the soil was depleted. There are large areas of agricultural Peru where attempts to apply modern imported technologies have had disastrous ecological consequences. In the jungle, where soil quality is poor, agricultural development is particularly problematic. So too with mining: the drive to maximise revenues in the short term typically obscures longer-term development planning. The concept of 'resource management' is conspicuously lacking; little thought is given to the needs of the next generation, still less to their heirs and descendants.

▼ Effluent flows from the mines at Toquepala and Cuajone. Communities lower down the valley complain of contaminated drinking water.

Susana Pastor

Mines, water, and the environment

You can smell the town of La Oroya before you see it. The last turn in the road reveals the smelter, its chimneys belching forth fumes into the already thin air. Situated at 3745 metres above sea level, and surrounded by bare limestone hills where the vegetation has long since died, La Oroya sits in bowl of concentrated gases, making this one of the least healthy places to live in Peru. Many of those who live and work in La Oroya suffer from chronic lung and bronchial disorders. The smelter was originally the nerve centre of the Cerro de Pasco Corporation's mining activities in the central *sierra*, until the Velasco government turned it into a state company, Centromin. It processes copper, silver, and zinc from the region's many individual mines. Deprived of investment since nationalisation, however, La Oroya has not improved with time. When the Fujimori government sought to privatise Centromin, its initial plans went awry because no large international mining company was prepared to assume La Oroya's environmental liabilities. In 1997, the government sold it off cheaply to a US firm, Doe Run, on the understanding that the firm would invest heavily in the upgrading of the plant. There are many doubts in the industry as to whether Doe Run has the money or the interest to do so.

The attempts of the Fujimori government to sell the state-owned mines and mining infrastructure coincided with moves to improve environmental regulation. In 1990, a new code was introduced to tighten controls. In many ways, it was quite advanced in its thinking. But the scale of the problem is huge. Peruvian mining operations have a poor environmental record. This is not just the case for former public sector mines, starved of investment from the 1970s onwards: it holds for private sector companies too. The SPCC copper refinery at Ilo vies with La Oroya as one of Peru's environmental black-spots. Since the enactment of the environment code, new investors in the mining industry have sought to incorporate its main points. However, this is no guarantee against environmental disasters, like the 1999 mercury spill at Choropampa, between the Yanacocha mine and the coast. The multinationals are not always the worst offenders; there are smaller Peruvian-owned firms that simply ignore the rules. But in the case of Choropampa, it turned out that there were no rules governing the transport of dangerous minerals and chemicals.

A major problem is the inability of the government to enforce the legislation. The National Environmental Council, the body ostensibly responsible, is a small organisation that lacks political force. In practice, the mining ministry itself regulates the industry. But the regulatory team at the ministry lacks the personnel and the funding to do the job properly. Its decisions also sit uneasily alongside the ministry's main mission to attract investment by whatever means possible. All projects have to undergo environmental impact assessments, but these are usually conducted by consultants at the behest of the companies involved. They are generally written in technical language that is difficult for non-experts and local people to understand. Consultation with local people is generally perfunctory, and objectors have little chance of making their voice heard. Local municipalities in mining areas, like those of Cajamarca and Huaraz, have taken the lead in pushing the government to take regulation more seriously.

Conflicts between mining companies and the communities that surround them are frequent. The main issues are usually land rights, and the compensation on offer for the use of land. Such payments rarely reflect the economic value of the land, and when objections are raised, the government can easily overrule them. The 1993 constitution revoked the clause in the previous constitution that made land inalienable. Without external help, communities are often powerless to defend their rights, and even when local NGOs become involved there is no guarantee of success.

ENVIRONMENTAL OFFENSIVE IN ILO

Susana Pastor

▲ *Ricardo Catacora and Gladys Márquez, technical staff at Labor.*

The town of Ilo has fought back against environmental pollution. Although the SPCC copper smelter continues to emit acrid black smoke, air pollution conditions in the town have improved. This is thanks largely to the activities of the town council and those of *Labor*, a dynamic local NGO that has lobbied locally and in Lima for better controls. As a result of such pressure, SPCC has taken steps to reduce emissions of sulphuric oxide from the smelter. In 1996, an official report said these were dangerously high. Since 1998, with the help of the Dutch government, the municipality has been monitoring air quality. In 2001, an epidemiological study was underway to measure the effects of pollution on human health in the town. The municipality has also tried to force SPCC to clean up a 15km stretch of beach, known locally as the 'Black Sea', where the sand is black from the smelter's residues. But it has been a tough struggle. According to Labor's Denis Rojas, the local council cannot assume responsibilities for such matters if the National Environment Council in Lima 'is nowhere to be seen'. The problem, he says, is that companies like SPCC have much better access to the highest levels of government than local people. This may be changing. With financial backing from the Inter-American Development Bank for better pollution control, the mining ministry is beginning to take environmental problems more seriously.

On occasions, however, international mining companies can be shamed into treating communities better. Complaints to the Australian mining ombudsman by Peruvian NGOs and communities, for instance, forced BHP-Billiton (an Anglo-Australian company with headquarters in Melbourne) to negotiate with the peasants' demands for compensation at Tintaya, the firm's mine in southern Peru.

Other causes of tension with local communities include the use of water and the contamination of rivers. Along the western side of the Andes, and through much of the highlands, rainfall is scarce (if not non-existent). In many places, mines take water from close to source, either to provide drinking water to the mining camps, or for use in the treatment and transport of minerals and waste. This causes water shortages lower down the river valleys, to the detriment of farmers who rely on rivers to irrigate their crops. In Moquegua, farmers have expressed concern that development of the Quellaveco mine by Anglo American will diminish the aquifer in the region, and exacerbate water shortages. Water courses also become polluted either as a result of spillages or, more commonly, from seepage of mine tailings into rivers and streams. For decades, the town of Locumba in the department of Tacna has suffered the effects of arsenic seeping into the river Ite from the Toquepala copper mine tailings. According to the mayor of Locumba, Juan Víctor Dávalos, contaminated water supplies have had a major long-term impact on the learning capacities of children in the town. At the point where the Ite runs out into the Pacific, between Ilo and Tacna, the environmental damage to

Annie Bungeroth

▲ *A key-ring produced by protestors at Tambo Grande reads, 'Trees are life, mines are death.'*

STATE WITHIN A STATE

They don't welcome passers-by in Toquepala. The entry point into the mine is guarded as if it were an international frontier, with guards checking and re-checking identity documents. SPCC, like other mining companies, is very averse to bad publicity from snooping journalists or NGO representatives. Beyond the checkpoint, visitors enter a different world. The managers' compound, at least, is like a piece of California relocated in the arid mountains of southern Peru. The street names are in English: Crystal Lane and Begonia Avenue. The mown lawns, the golf course, and the tennis courts suggest no water shortage or poisoning here. Together with the smelter at Ilo, and the copper mine of Cuajone, near Moquegua – all connected by the company railway – SPCC is like a state within a state. Commercial calculations are uppermost on SPCC's agenda, especially as copper prices decline. Although SPCC pays its staff well by Peruvian mining standards, the payroll has diminished as machines progressively replace people. Toquepala, Cuajone, and Ilo employ 5000 workers, and a further 2500 depend on tertiary firms providing services. Ten years ago, SPCC employed twice as many workers. The region's economy has certainly felt the difference.

vegetation is clear for all to see, in spite of recent steps by SPCC to clean up the shoreline.

Water shortage in much of Peru has sharpened conflicts between agricultural producers, large and small, over the ownership of, and access to, water courses. This is far from being just a problem related to mining. Changes in the flow of rivers can have major implications for farmers. When the San Lorenzo dam was constructed on the Quiroz River in Piura in the 1950s, it cut the flow of water into the Piura River, reducing the amounts available to cotton-growers in the lower Piura region. The angry response of the estate owners led to Velasco building a canal to channel water from the Chira River (where it is plentiful the year round) into the Piura (where it is scarce for much of the year). Water is life on the coastal strip, and nothing grows without it. However, water is often used wastefully. The cultivation of rice over large areas of the otherwise arid department of Lambayeque – involving intensive use of water – is inappropriate where water has to be transported from the *sierra*, and where the end result is salinisation. The cost of hugely expensive irrigation systems, borne by the state, is not factored into the price of the end-product. In the *sierra*, too, access to water is of

▶ *The Piura river-crossing into Tambo Grande – in the rains it becomes completely submerged, and travellers must cross by boat.*

Susana Pastor

fundamental importance to agriculture, since water is scarce for much of the year, and drought is not uncommon. Access to water, as well as access to land, is the source of ancestral conflicts within and between communities, and between communities and major landowners.

Natural disasters

The Spanish *conquistadores* had a special gift for building cities in places prone to natural disasters: Mexico City, Guatemala City, Bogotá, Quito, Lima, Santiago all lie abreast a major fissure that arcs around the Pacific rim, giving rise to earthquakes and volcanoes. Peru has had its fair share of natural disasters, the worst in living memory being the 1970 earthquake which claimed 70,000 victims. Some 20,000 alone died in the town of Yungay in Ancash. The earthquake set off avalanches and a mudslide down the side of Huascarán (Peru's highest mountain), which buried the town. All that remains of where Yungay once stood is the tips of the four palm trees that had stood at each corner of the main square. It is a poignant monument to the power of nature to wreak havoc on unsuspecting people.

Susana Pastor

▲ *Jocelyn and Luzbenia's school in Locumba collapsed during the Arequipa earthquake. They are studying in temporary classrooms.*

The most powerful recent earthquake was the 2001 quake in Arequipa. Measuring 7.2 on the Richter scale, it produced large-scale damage, and shook the whole of southern Peru. Its tremors were felt as far away as Cochabamba in Bolivia. One of the worst-affected areas was Moquegua, where the geology is particularly unstable. There, 15 people were killed and many hundreds made homeless. At Ilo, people feared that the earthquake would bring in its wake a *tsunami*, or tidal wave, that would swamp the town. In the event, it did not happen, but in this well-organised town, schoolchildren are drilled in what to do in the event of such a calamity. In Camaná, further north up the coast, a *tsunami* destroyed nearly 1000 homes.

Among the worst-hit towns was Locumba in Tacna department. Situated in the desert, 95 per cent of the houses there were either destroyed or made uninhabitable. Even the town's stout church – a holy shrine marking the spot where Christ appeared in a vision to a local peasant – was badly shaken. Electricity and water supplies were cut, and road communications to Tacna severed, when the bridge that carries the Panamerican Highway collapsed into the Ite river. Although the immediate response from the authorities was slow and half-hearted, international aid agencies responded to Locumba's plight rapidly, providing temporary shelter and cisterns to store water. After the initial emergency, the municipality of Locumba faced the daunting challenge of reconstruction. But the mayor of Locumba struck an optimistic note when he described how the disaster had elicited a spirit of mutual self-help and solidarity among the townspeople. He claimed that out of the rubble and debris, a new, better-planned town would emerge, more resilient to future tremors. 'We start again from scratch,' he says, 'putting in things like proper drains and sewers we never had before.'

Tremors are a fairly common feature of everyday life in Lima and other cities, and a reminder that one day the 'big one' (*el grande*) may strike. The biggest quake to affect the city was in 1940; but then Lima had a population of 400,000, not eight million as now.

The possibility of a major earthquake in Lima is a nightmare scenario for urban planners. In theory, tall buildings in the capital are built to withstand earth movements. In practice, safe construction techniques add to the cost of building, and are only ever applied in higher-income neighbourhoods where local councils check on compliance. The regulations governing medium-rise housing are less strict than for high-rise, and the majority of city housing falls into this category. Most houses and public sector buildings in Lima are constructed by builders whose main concern is to erect walls and roofs as quickly and cheaply as possible. The collapse of a school in Nazca revealed the fact that the builder, to cut costs, had skimped on the metal ties that grip the iron rods sustaining the concrete beams and pillars.

PREDES is an NGO that specialises in disaster prevention and mitigation. It helps to diagnose risk levels in communities, and develops contingency plans with local municipalities and grass-roots organisations. It is slow, unspectacular work, but is advancing well. Real problems arise

Constantino Condori and Justina Velarde Condori saw their home in Piñapa, just outside Locumba, fold up like a house of cards. Constantino had been living in a tent for months when we talked to him. He described how, with the quake, the whole landscape seemed to move, and the valley was filled with choking dust as rock pounded down the hillsides. 'It only lasted a few minutes,' he said, 'but it seemed to last for ever.' Constantino rents a few hectares of land close to the river Ite. The year before, most of his crops were washed away as unusually heavy rains in the *sierra* turned this modest river into a roaring torrent.

The picture shows Constantino and Justina outside their newly-built house, one of 79 self-construct housing modules donated to Locumba by Oxfam.

when poverty forces people to settle on land that is ever more exposed to risk, for instance, steep hillsides where even small earth movements set off avalanches of rock and stones. According to Gilberto Romero, 'You can take steps to build walls of stones but, fundamentally, you cannot de-link preventative work from strategies to improve living conditions.' A key element in the ability of people to survive natural disasters is the strength of community organisation, and the existence of preventative strategies that cut across all other social programmes. 'The strength of community organisation in Lima is very unequal', says Gilberto. 'For historical reasons, it is much stronger in some neighbourhoods than others.'

Earthquakes apart, the other most common type of natural disaster in Peru is *El Niño*, the meteorological phenomenon that regularly plays havoc with rainfall along the length of the Peruvian coast and in the *sierra*. The precise causes of *Niños* are still not well-understood, but there is no doubt as to the symptoms. The cold waters that normally flow up the coast of Peru from the Antarctic are displaced by warmer waters flowing south from the tropics. The rise in sea temperature is usually first noticed by fishermen who see their catch diminish as a result. *El Niño* brings rain to areas (like the *costa*) where it never normally rains, and drought to areas (like the *sierra*) where there is usually plentiful seasonal rainfall. As a result it can have catastrophic effects on both fishing and agriculture. *Niño* years tend to be cyclical, happening at about five-year intervals. However, predicting the strongest *Niño* years is more difficult. The worst *Niño* years in the 20th century were 1925, 1983, and 1997-98. Meteorologists have predicted a return of the *Niño* in 2003. Perhaps all that can be deduced from this is that, with global warming, bad *Niños* may be becoming

▼ This bridge across the Rio Bigote in Piura was built to replace one that was washed away during the 1997 El Niño. The destruction of the bridge left thousands of people cut off.

Annie Bungeroth

Annie Bungeroth

▲ The *Niño* rains destroyed the bamboo roofs of houses.

▼ A woodcutter chops trees washed down from the mountains during El Niño. He will use them as firewood.

more frequent. Also problematic is *La Niña*, which follows *El Niño* but with reverse effects.

When the 1983 *Niño* struck, it had dramatic affects in both the *costa* and *sierra*. There were no preparations to mitigate its worst effects. Swollen rivers along the Pacific coast burst their banks, creating widespread flooding. Houses are typically made of mud, without proper roofs, and were unable to withstand the damage. In many places, houses, roads, and bridges were simply washed away. The drought that year throughout the *sierra* was visually less dramatic than the coastal flooding, but worse in its economic impact on the peasant economy. The experience of 1983, though, had the positive effect of encouraging many communities to take steps to minimise the risks in future.

The early warning signals of *El Niño* events are various, and often reflect popular lore: the appearance of herons in the *sierra* betokens drought; the appearance of frogs, imminent rainfall. Whatever the chosen indicator, *Niños* are to some extent predictable, enabling pre-emptive action to take place. When the *Niño* returned in 1997, the people of Piura – to name but one instance – were better prepared than in 1983. Unfortunately, the municipal and regional authorities had failed to co-ordinate their actions, and the city was flooded. The Fujimori government was unwilling to work with NGOs, and thus failed to take advantage of the advances in local organisation which could have been used to harness people's energies in a co-ordinated manner.

In Lima, PREDES also works in contingency planning to reduce the dangers of climatic variations on human settlements. Other than earthquakes, the main problems are flooding and landslides. Within the Rimac river basin, inland from Lima, these problems occur during most years, though the effects are magnified in *Niño* years. Effective responses to such problems are often blocked by bureaucratic obstacles, such as the number of different institutions involved, and their failure to co-ordinate their actions. The boundaries between municipalities do not necessarily conform to geographical logic, and within a single river basin there may be several mayors working in opposition to each other. One of PREDES' main contributions has been to create spaces in which different local agencies can collaborate. It also tries to inculcate greater awareness of such problems among government ministries and agencies. However, as Gilberto Romero remarks, this is problematic since, 'Such overlapping notions still do not fit with ministerial responsibilities.'

Conclusion

▲ *Lima construction workers take a break. But how can Peruvians build a better future for their country?*

Looking at Peru in terms of the 'macro' picture, you may be forgiven for feeling a little depressed. Politically, the country has swung between authoritarian and rather more democratic forms of government, but without breaking the pattern of elite control. Although citizens may use their vote to determine who should be president or who should represent them in Congress, the extent to which ordinary people can use these rights to 'empower' themselves is still very limited. The size of the gap between rich and poor is such that the economically powerful and politically influential will fight tooth and nail to maintain their privileges, even if this means resorting to undemocratic methods. Democratic institutions are weakly constituted in Peru. Equally, the rate of economic growth has been sluggish over the last thirty years, and the distribution of its benefits has continued to favour a small proportion of the population at the expense of the great majority. For most people, living standards have tended to decline, while the country continues to export a good proportion of its wealth in the form of debt repayment. Poverty and inequality have become more pronounced. The chances of the average 18-year old getting a reasonably-paid job today are much slimmer than would have been the case at the end of the 1960s or the beginning of the 1970s.

Look at Peru in 'micro' terms, and you get a rather different, less pessimistic picture. In researching for this book, we interviewed many people who do not form part of the elite: slum dwellers in Lima, peasant farmers in highland Ayacucho, coffee growers in Piura, mineworkers in Tacna and Moquegua, and jungle Indians in the department of San Martín. We also spoke with many of those who work with ordinary people to help them resolve some of the problems they face. Undaunted by the political and economic processes going on around them, people exhibit enormous energy and creativity in building for the future, both at the family and community levels. They may be poor, but they are determinedly resourceful. One of Peru's greatest assets is the strength of its community organisation. Whether working alone or supported by NGOs, such organisation provides a response to unfavourable circumstances. Often, it is the only way forward. During my travels, I was struck not just by the resilience of those I met, but also by their determination to ensure a better future for their sons and daughters.

This book was written at a time when democratic institutions were beginning to be rebuilt after a decade of authoritarian rule. The people I met were hopeful that democracy would provide them with some of the tools they need to improve their situation. Democratic institutions should make it easier for them to organise and press for change, providing some defence against repression, whether at the local, regional, or national level. No longer are political institutions manipulated by a national intelligence machine. The power of the armed forces seems to be in check. Past abuses of power and privilege are under investigation, and people I met were hopeful that the lifting of impunity would send a powerful message to the country's new rulers. Money for community development, it was hoped, will no longer be tied to support for the government in office. Voted in on the slogan '*más trabajo*' (more work), the new government promised to tackle the chronic problem of inadequate employment. Perhaps most importantly of all, it has promised to undertake a fundamental shake-up of the way the country is governed, devolving power to local government. This offers the prospect of real 'empowerment', a major change in a country accustomed to top-down government directed from the National Palace in Lima. Perhaps more than ever before, people were concerned with human rights – including citizen rights, labour rights, women's rights – and how to establish and defend them.

▶ *Peace is bringing many changes to Ayacucho – including the Internet.*

Susana Pastor

While pleased by such political changes, most people are somewhat sceptical about how much greater democracy will really help them. Democracy has proved wanting in the recent past. In the 1980s, hopes that the end of military rule would lead to a better future proved misplaced. That decade ended in a spiral of political violence and hyperinflation. As in the 1980s, the ability of government to raise incomes and generate employment continues to be held in check by the dictates of the IMF and foreign creditors. Policies such as privatisation, applauded in Washington, have received a less than rapturous welcome from those threatened with having to pay more for essential services, or those at risk of losing their jobs. Both the IMF and the World Bank have made no secret of their distaste for policy agendas other than their own, especially those considered 'populist'.

As in other Latin American countries and indeed further afield, most people continue to have little faith in politicians of whatever persuasion. Opinion polls attest to the low esteem in which politicians of all sorts are held. Peru's 'political class' has hardly distinguished itself over the previous 30 years for its long-term vision, its capacity to get things done, or its resistance to the economic temptations of high office. The 1970s military governments were hated by the popular movement and the business class alike. The Belaunde and García governments both dissipated the high expectations they initially generated. García's regime ended in total discredit in 1990, seen both as incompetent and corrupt. The Fujimori government, itself a product of public aversion to conventional parties, was finally hounded from office in November 2000. It was possibly the most politically devious and corrupt administration in Peru's republican history.

Hence the new preoccupation with participation, transparency, and respect for rights. Yet, popular organisation is not immune from corruption or manipulation, even in more democratic times. Similarly, local government can be as unaccountable and opaque as national government. Still, the interviews on which this book are based suggest that popular organisation provides the key to establishing and defending rights, and that effective decentralisation should help 'lock in' these gains at the local level. Governments will tend to remain indifferent to the plight of the poor unless forced to do otherwise. For things to change, then, the myriad of grass-roots organisations of different types need to make their voices heard. Building citizenship is a slow, difficult process. But as Luzmila in San Juan de Lurigancho says, 'We take it step by step.... The secret is that we are all united, that we trust one another.'

Annie Bungeroth

▲ *A girl eavesdrops on a women's group meeting in San Juan de Bigote, Piura.*

Facts and figures

Land area
1.3 million sq km (the third largest country in South America)

Population
26.7 million (2002 est.); growth rate: 1.5 per cent pa

Urban population
72.1 per cent (2001)

Main cities
Lima 7.7 million inhabitants; Arequipa 663,000; Trujillo 620,000

Average life expectancy
69.7 years (2002): men 67.2 years; women 72.3 years

Infant mortality
33 per 1000 live births

Child malnutrition
22.9 per cent (under 5s, by size for age, 2000)

Poverty
54.8 per cent of the population lives in poverty (2001), and 24.4 per cent in extreme poverty. In rural areas, 51.3 per cent live in extreme poverty.

Inequality
31.9 per cent of income goes to 10 per cent of households (2000); Gini coefficient (1999) 46.2

Urban employment
49.7 per cent of labour force employed (2000); unemployment 7.4 per cent; sub-employment 42.9 per cent

Housing
Homes with piped water 71.4 per cent (2000); with access to sewerage within the home 58.8 per cent

Literacy
Illiteracy rate 7.2 per cent (2000); among women in the rural *sierra* 25.2 per cent

Healthcare
17.9 hospital beds per 10,000 inhabitants (1996); 10.3 doctors per 10,000 inhabitants

Gross Domestic Product
US$ 53.6 billion (2000); US$ 2091 per capita

Average annual growth (1996-2001)
2.15 per cent

Major economic activities
Agriculture (7.6 per cent of GDP); mining and oil (4.7 per cent); manufacturing (16 per cent); commerce (14.6 per cent); services (39.2 per cent)

Foreign debt
US$ 27.7 billion; budget for debt service (2002): US$ 2 billion; budget for education: US$ 540 million; budget for health: US$ 370 million

Exports
US$ 7.03 billion (2000); main exports: minerals (copper, gold, zinc, silver), fishmeal, coffee, textiles

Imports
US$ 7.35 billion (2000)

Foreign investment
Spain (US$ 2.4 billion), UK (US$ 1.9 billion), USA (US$ 1.9 billion) (2000)

Currency
The Sol; average exchange rate (2000): 3.49 soles = US$1.00

Dates and events

11,000 BC Earliest remains of human settlement in coastal Peru

800 BC The beginnings of the Chavín culture in the northern highlands

600 AD Tiahuanaco and Wari cultures flourish in southern Peru

1400 The beginnings of Inca imperial expansion

1532 Arrival of the first Spanish *conquistadores* in Peru under Francisco Pizarro

1780-82 Rebellion of Túpac Amaru II

1821 Proclamation of the independence of Peru, following San Martín's invasion

1824 Battle of Ayacucho and final defeat of Spanish armies

1879-83 War of the Pacific, in which Peru loses Arica and Tarapacá to Chile

1895 Nicolas de Piérola becomes president; initiation of the 'aristocratic republic'

1919 Augusto Leguía becomes president, initiating the 'oncenio'

1930 Death of José Carlos Mariátegui

1932 Suppression of the APRA (*Alianza Popular Revolucionaria Americana*) Trujillo rising; APRA outlawed

1932-33 Border war with Colombia

1941 Border war with Ecuador

1948 Coup brings General Odría to power; APRA outlawed

1963 Election of Fernando Belaunde

1968 Belaunde toppled by General Juan Velasco

1969 Agrarian reform decreed

1975 Velasco replaced by more conservative General Francisco Morales Bermúdez

1979 Enactment of new constitution; vote granted to illiterate people

1980 Election victory of Fernando Belaunde; initiation of armed struggle by *Sendero Luminoso*

1983 *El Niño* crisis; left-wing victory in Lima mayoral elections

1984 Peru defaults on part of its foreign debt

1985 Election victory of Alan García and APRA; debt servicing limited to 10 per cent of annual exports

1986 Massacre of Sendero prisoners in three Lima jails

1990 Election of Alberto Fujimori as president

1992 Fujimori's *autogolpe* and the closure of Congress; capture of Abimael Guzmán

1993 New constitution enacted, allowing Fujimori's immediate re-election

1995 Fujimori re-elected for a second term; border war with Ecuador

1997 Japanese embassy siege, following MRTA hostage-taking

1997-98 *El Niño* crisis

2000 Fujimori re-elected in fraudulent election; election bribery scandal; Fujimori driven into exile in Japan; interim administration of Valentín Paniagua

2001 Alejandro Toledo elected president; new Congress elected

Sources and further reading

Bowen, Sally (2000) *The Fujimori File: Peru and its President 1990-2000*, Lima: Peru Monitor

Cameron, Maxwell and Philip Mauceri (eds.) (1997) *The Peruvian Labyrinth: Polity, Society, Economy*, University Park PA: Penn State Press

Crabtree, John (1992) *Peru under García: An Opportunity Lost*, Basingstoke: Macmillan

Crabtree, John and Jim Thomas (eds.) (1998) *Fujimori's Peru: The Political Economy*, London: ILAS

Gorriti, Gustavo (1999) *The Shining Path: A History of the Millenarian War in Peru*, Chapel Hill: North Carolina University Press

Holligan, Jane (1998) *Peru in Focus*, London: Latin America Bureau

Klaren, Peter (2000) *Peru: Society and Nationhood in the Andes*, Oxford and New York: OUP

Poole, Deborah and Gerardo Renique (1992) *Peru: Time of Fear*, London: Latin American Bureau

Scott Palmer, David (1992) *Shining Path of Peru*, New York: Saint Martin's Press

Sheahan, John (1999) *Searching for a Better Society: The Peruvian Economy since 1950*, University Park PA: Penn State Press

Starn, Orin, Carlos Iván Degregori, and Robin Kirk (eds.) (1995) *The Peru Reader*, Durham NC and London: Duke University Press

Stern, Steve (ed.) (1998) *Shining and Other Paths: War and Society in Peru, 1980-1995*, Durham NC and London: Duke University Press

Thorp, Rosemary and Geoffrey Bertram (1978) *Peru: 1870-1977*, London and Basingstoke: Macmillan

Susana Pastor

Sources and websites

Amnesty International, http:// www.amnesty.org
Various reports on the human rights
situation in Peru

Asociación Pro Derechos Humanos (Aprodeh),
http://www.aprodeh.org.pe
Many publications, with an emphasis on
human rights

Caretas, http://www.caretas.com.pe
Weekly magazine, usually with a fairly
critical focus

Cuánto: Perú en Números, e-mail:
cuanto@terra.com.pe
This is the best available compendium of
statistics about Peru.

Ideele, http://www.idl.org.pe
Magazine of the Instituto de Defensa Legal
(IDL), with a focus on the defence of rights

Instituto de Estudios Peruanos (IEP),
http://iep.perucultural.org.pe
Centre for research and publications over a
wide range of themes, both contemporary
and historical

Instituto Nacional de Estadística e Informática
(INEI), http://www.inei.gob.pe
Statistics and analysis of a wide range of
social and economic problems

La República, http://www.larepublica.com.pe
One of Peru's better newspapers

LANIC Peru,
http://www.lanic.utexas.edu/la/peru
Produced by the University of Texas, this is
one of the most comprehensive portals to
information on all things Peruvian.

Peru Support Group,
http://www.perusupportgroup.co.uk
UK-based information/lobbying agency.
Produces bimonthly Peru Update as well as
other publications (recent publications on
women, political developments, human
rights, and the debt problem).

Quehacer, http:// www.desco.org.pe
Bimonthly publication covering current
political, economic, and cultural
developments, produced by DESCO (Centro
de Estudios y Promoción del Desarrollo –
Centre for the Study and Promotion of
Development).

▼ *The second day of the Pérez family fiesta begins with a
procession, and a mass in the recently-constructed family chapel.*

Susana Pastor

Oxfam in Peru

Measured in terms of its resources, Peru is an immensely rich country. But measured by the living standards of its population, it is immensely poor. The majority of Peruvians participate in informal and imperfect markets; they have minimal participation in the public decisions that affect their lives; and they are vulnerable to the effects of natural disasters and of the recent armed conflict.

Oxfam GB has been working in Peru for over 30 years. Oxfam GB works with local organisations to reduce people's vulnerability to disasters. We do this through the creation of disaster preparedness plans, and through ensuring the inclusion of risk analyses in local development plans. Over the past year, Oxfam GB has been working with other humanitarian organisations to develop a strategy to increase the exchange of information and co-ordination between humanitarian actors in Peru, including the Peruvian government.

Oxfam GB co-ordinates with and supports human rights organisations working with the populations of Ayacucho and Huánuco, which were affected by the political violence during the 1980s and 1990s. The work aims to capture lessons arising from the recovery and restitution of human rights to the affected populations, a process beginning with the work of the National Truth and Reconciliation Commission, from mid-2001 onwards.

Oxfam GB supports a number of long-term initiatives aimed at the empowerment of poor Peruvian citizens. Oxfam GB's work in this area is focused on building accountability. We support grass-roots NGOs in undertaking monitoring projects focusing on public policies and programmes, such as the national food assistance programme. We are also supporting similar activities, organised by local governments in rural areas, to develop participatory planning, transparency in public management, and accountability.

Oxfam GB supports the *Red Perú*, a group of about 150 *mesas de concertación*. The *mesas* constitute spaces for participatory planning, and in a few cases, for the management of local development. They typically bring public authorities and representatives of social organisations together, generating a process of local consultation. Oxfam GB also works with the *Asociación National de Centros*, the national network of NGOs, to support the National Conference on Social Development, the major space where representatives of Peru's civil society groups meet.

Over the next five years, Oxfam has received funding from the UK Department for International Development in order to develop and manage a programme aimed at ensuring access to human rights for poor

Susana Pastor

Susana Pastor

people. Of the US$10 million allocated to the project, $6.5 million will constitute a fund for the support of locally-managed projects, based in the Andean region of southern Peru, to promote poor people's ability to exercise their basic rights.

Support for sustainable livelihoods forms another major part of Oxfam GB's work in Peru. In rural areas, this developing programme will focus on the national agrarian policies affecting small-scale producers. By focusing on producers' access to productive assets, and on their ability to produce and market their products, this programme is intended to ensure that poor people have increasing power within markets. In Lima, a future urban programme will support strategies intended to create sustainable livelihoods, building on the experiences of several major urban NGOs with which Oxfam GB has worked for many years. In addition, Oxfam GB will implement a programme aimed at the improvement of working conditions for women in key economic sectors, such as agro-export.

In each of these areas of intervention, Oxfam GB co-ordinates closely with the other members of Oxfam International currently working in Peru: Intermón, Novib, Oxfam America, Oxfam Canada, and Oxfam Solidarité. This co-ordination has been particularly focused around humanitarian response to the June 2001 earthquake in southern Peru. It has also been important in Tambo Grande, where the struggle between civil society, industry, and the government has become a symbol of the struggle of thousands of citizens to have their views taken into account in public decision-making on issues affecting their lives and livelihoods.

Acknowledgements

Thanks go to those of Oxfam's partner organisations that I visited, and those who work with them. They went to great lengths to welcome me and to share their views and experiences with me. Their enthusiasm and perseverance are an inspiration. Thanks also to the staff of the Oxfam office in Lima, particularly Martín Beaumont, Ana María Rebaza, and Zorobabel Cancino for their meticulous planning of the visits. Susi Pastor, the photographer, was an excellent travelling companion for the three weeks we were 'on the road' in Piura, Ayacucho, Tacna as well as in many different parts of Lima. Thanks to Martín Beaumont, Constantino Casabuenas, Judith Condor, Isabel Crabtree-Condor, and Lewis Taylor for their comments on the text. Kate Kilpatrick, my editor, provided much encouragement and support as well as exacting deadlines. I would also like to thank Fidelina Vidal, my mother-in-law, who didn't mind her house being treated as a hotel for the time I was in Lima.

John Crabtree

Index

national identity 17
nationalisation 2, 26, 36
Nazca lines 5
neo-liberalism 40–50

ochenio 25
Odría, Manuel 25, 26
oil industry see hydrocarbon industry
oncenio 25
OPEC 37
opium 54

Pacific Ocean 7–8
Paniagua, Valentín
participatory planning 34
Partido Popular Cristiano (PPC) 27
party political system 27–8
patriarchy 11
pharmacies 66
Plan Colombia 53
police 56, 59–60
    corruption 54, 59
    reform 60
political corruption 21, 24–5, 27, 40,
    82
political protest 25
political reforms 25–6, 32–4
political system 22, 25–28, 32–4
political violence 18–19, 27, 28–30,
    50–4, 55–8, 82
pollution
    air 32, 71, 72–4
    water 74
popular participation in government
    34, 80–2
population policy 66–7
potatoes 47, 48
poverty 10–11, 12–13, 45, 80–2
poverty, extreme 45
pre-Columbian civilisations 3–4, 5
pregnancy 67
pressure groups 26
price adjustment 40
prison system 58
private health insurance 64
privatisation 40–1, 46, 82
public investment 7
public sector 43, 73
public spending 11, 45, 62, 63

Quechua 3, 17

radio, community 24
railways 1
Raimondi, Antonio 1
rainforest 9
rape 56, 67
regional politics 4
religion, role of 16
religious festivals 15–16
reproductive health 66–7
resource management 70–6
respiratory illness 72
rice 48, 75
river valleys 7, 8, 9
rondas campesinas 30
rubber industry 36
rural development 11, 64
rural-urban migration 18–19, 48, 49

Sacsahuamán 3
school-building 61–2
Sendero Luminoso 19, 28–30, 31,
    50–4, 55–8
shanty towns 18–19, 30–1
silver 8, 72
sinchis 56
social change 13, 61
social organisation 3, 29
social security 43
social structure 10–11, 61, 68
Spain 1, 31
Spanish Empire 4
SPCC (Southern Peru Copper
    Corporation) 32, 73–5
sterilisation 67
structural adjustment 40–50
sugar industry 7, 36
sulphur dioxide 32
sustainable development 71–2
SUTEP 62, 63

Tambo Grande 70–6
taxation 47
teachers 62
terracing 4
terrorism 57
tertiary education 62
theatre 17
Toledo, Alejandro 25, 34, 42, 45, 55,
    60, 62, 65, 69
torture 56
trade barriers 41
trade unions 43–5
Truth and Reconciliation
    Commission 55, 58
tsunamis 76

under-employment 12
unemployment 12, 43–5, 80–1
United Kingdom 1
United States of America 1, 19–20,
    25, 35, 50, 52–4
urban conflict 31, 59–60
urban development 10–11, 30–1, 64,
    77–9
urban expansion 18–19, 48, 59–60
Uruguay 25
USAID 52

Vargas Llosa, Mario 22
Velasco, Juan 25, 26, 30, 36
Venezuela 4
Vietnam 53
Vildoso, Carmen 44
Villa El Salvador 30–1
'Vladivideos' 21
volcanoes 76
voting rights 2

wage levels 42
War of the Pacific 4
waste management 32
water pollution 2, 74–6
water resources 5, 7, 9
water resources, access to 71, 74–6
wheat 48
women
    employment 43, 44, 46, 49
    and girls, education of 10–11, 62
    politics, and public life 10, 31,
        33–4, 46, 65–7
    position of 10–11, 17, 65–7
    violence against 33, 67
women's rights 65–7
workers' rights 43–5
World Bank 36, 39–40, 61, 70, 82

Yuyachkani theatre group 17

zinc 72